Which Way Is UP:
How To Survive In A Down Economy

A quick reference guide on how to earn quick cash, save money, and invest in times of economic hardship.

If you are searching for a way to regain your financial stability and independence, pay your children's college education, purchase a home without losing it, start a business, purchase government assets at wholesale prices, retire peacefully; or simply looking to earn quick cash, this book is for you!

IWIN BOOK PUBLISHING AND PRODUCTION COMPANY
P.O. Box 3293, N.W., Washington, D.C. 20010

Library of Congress Catalog Card Number: 2010934589
ISBN: 9780615393728
Barcode: 0615393721

FIRST EDITION
Edited By: Irene Warren
Printed in the United States of America

PREFACE

This book is not a get-rich quick guide, nor is it intended to offer any legal advice. This book is based on research and Irene's personal testimony, in which she shares a few common sense principles and investment strategies in how to earn quick cash, as a way to survive economic hardship.

This book was written to inspire entrepreneurs, those who desire to start a business, as well as business professionals desiring to earn and save money, as they operate their companies. Also, this book was written for the average American citizen desiring to better manage their finances and everyday households.

In short, this book will enlighten you about entrepreneurship ventures, various financial resources that might be available to you, and introduce laws that can possibly assist you in regaining your financial stability.

If you are searching for ways to regain your financial independence, pay your children's college education, prepare a hefty nest egg for your retirement, purchase a home; or simply searching for ways to avoid foreclosure, while learning savvy business tips, this book is for you!

ACKNOWLEDGEMENTS

First, I would like to thank my Lord and Savior, Jesus Christ for leading me in the right direction. Second, I would like to thank Mr. Bego, a successful businessman and entrepreneur in his own right for his support in making it possible to publish this book. Also, I am very grateful that I am an American citizen and that I live in a country that encourages capitalism, welcomes opportunity, upholds freedom and civil liberties, which have all played a major role in helping me to pursue my dreams and to take captive the pursuit of happiness. To my son, Quentin, thank you.

Praises for "Which Way Is Up"

Irene Warren is the epitome of a true American heroine. While she understands and values the fundamental proposition that all Americans are guaranteed the "unalienable rights" of life, liberty, and the pursuit of happiness, she also understands the limits of these guarantees. In our current society, where everyone is seemingly looking for the next government handout or speaking of that to which they are "entitled," Irene has realized that there is no substitute for hard work, faith in God, family values, accountability, responsibility, character, ethics, self-dependence and preservation. Unfortunately, these values that once constituted the backbone of our country are conspicuously absent in today's world. Like many of us, Irene has lived through good times and bad. She has persevered without depending on her government to get by. Instead, through her own ingenuity, she utilized the free market system to persevere through the tough times. We need more Americans like Irene -- those who will depend on themselves, and not on government entitlements! With this book, Irene not only gives a glimpse of how she has persevered, but also provides the rest of us with a road map to self-sufficiency. Hooray for Irene!

David A. Bego, Author: The Devil at My Doorstep

Please visit Dave's blog at http://devilatmydoorstep.wordpress.com or comment about his book at http://www.facebook.com/pages/Devil-at-My-Doorstep/102244393150647.

CONTENTS

Page

INTRODUCTION

I was inspired to write this book, so others experiencing economic hardship would know they are not alone in their struggle to attain financial freedom and also share with others that there is a way out, but only if they arm themselves with the knowledge needed to do so.

I have come to the realization what God says in Hosea 4:6 is true:

"My people perish from a lack of knowledge."

One thing that kept me going in times of despair is that I refused to stop dreaming. My dreams were all I had left after experiencing economic hardship. However, I had to get over beating myself up and asking myself, why did this happen to me? I remember thinking, "I am a good person: I pay my taxes, I don't drink, I don't gamble, and I am a law-abiding citizen, so why is this happening to a good person like me?" After months of feeling sorry for myself, I came to the realization that this type of thinking is not only unhealthy, but it is so far from the truth. Unfortunately, misfortunes happen to good people just like you and me every day.

Sorry to say, even when we plan our lives right and manage to make all the right choices, life still, sometimes can let us down. We tell our children; go to school, graduate college, work hard, obey the law, and treat people right and life will be just grand! Except, we fail to take into consideration a thing called fate, which is a predestined pathway that leads us into destiny.

Life, as many already know, is full of growing pains, adversity, ups and downs, and can often times bring us a world of disappointment. However, we can take comfort in knowing that we live in the freest and richest country in the world, where dreams are birthed and become someone's reality every day. Therefore, beloved, we must keep in mind that America is a place where all things are possible, if we continue to believe in ourselves and hold strong to our faith.

My advice to you is this, "Never stop dreaming, because life is always worth living no matter what we might be facing." Remember, tomorrow is another day that brings forth hope and allows us another opportunity to try again. So, I say enjoy living again, as you get busy building.

Edgar Allan Poe once said, "Those who dream by day are cognizant of many things that escape those who dream only at night."

Photo: Public Domain- An unidentified portrait of <u>Edgar Allan Poe</u>: photographed at the <u>University of Virginia</u> in 1913.

Chapter One
An Idle Mind Is The Devil's Workshop
(By H. G. Bohn, "Hand-Book of Proverbs," 1855)

Protecting Your Ideas And Inventions
This chapter covers the following topics:
*How To Draft A Non-Disclosure Agreement
*How To Register A Copyright With The Library Of Congress
*How To Draft A Poor Man's Copyright
*How To Register A Trademark
*How To File A Patent Registration

Although we live in a country that welcomes creativity, entrepreneurship, and freedom of expression, we still have to protect our ideas and creative works from being stolen. In my opinion, the first step in protecting a work is to draft a non-disclosure agreement, prior to disclosing our ideas to a second or third party.

What Is A Non-Disclosure Agreement?
A non-disclosure agreement is a legal agreement between two or more parties who share confidential information for a specific purpose. A non-disclosure agreement should specify any limitations in usage of the sensitive information. Also, a non-disclosure agreement should address who or if, anyone else should have access to the sensitive material. In addition, a non-disclosure agreement should outline the necessary steps, in which all parties have agreed to take in order to protect sensitive material from falling into the hands of unauthorized persons, or from falling into the public domain. In short, a non-disclosure agreement establishes the ownership of an idea.

Who Should Draft A Non-Disclosure Agreement?
Those persons who have created or invented something and also, those who have authored a literary work should consider drafting a non-disclosure agreement. Still today, a non-disclosure agreement is one of the most affordable and easiest ways to protect trade secrets,

or creative works.

How Does A Non-Disclosure Agreement Work?
Generally, a non-disclosure agreement is governed by state statues. However, to ensure that your idea and/or creative work is protected to the fullest extinct of the law, one should seek council from an attorney, prior to sharing an idea, or creation with anyone.

An Important Note
Having a meeting or discussion about your creative work without legal protection constitutes public disclosure.

What Should A Basic Non-Disclosure Agreement Include?
A basic non-disclosure agreement should include the following sections: The purpose, a definition, the disclosure of the confidential material, the person's name that is claiming ownership of the idea; or the creative works. Also, the agreement should include a return of materials section, an intellectual property rights section, an independent development section, a term of agreement section, a miscellaneous section, as well as a remedy and notice section. For educational purposes only, the author has provided a couple of examples and web links for those who desire to draft a non-disclosure agreement. To view samples, please visit http://www.score.org/downloads/NonDisclosureAgreement.pdf or http://tradesecretshomepage.com/form1.html.

What Is Intellectual Property?
There are three types intellectual property
*Copyrights
*Patents
*Trademarks

What Is A Copyright?
Under (Title 17, U.S. Code) of the United States, a copyright is a type of intellectual property that protects all original forms of literary, musical, artistic, and architectural works. A Copyright protects artistic expressions, such as novels, poems, biographies, songs, compositions, translations,

atlases, and other original works of authorship. Also, the creation of websites and computer programs are protected under copyright law.
In short, a copyright is a legal and binding document that protects authors who have created an original work.

What Is Not Protected Under Copyright Law?
*Titles
*Ideas
*Facts

An Important Note
Under Copyright law, a copyrighted work cannot be copied, reproduced, distributed or publicly displayed without the consent of the author or copyright owner. Copyrights are designed to prove ownership of an original creative work. Therefore, to prevent plagiarism and theft of your creation, it is wise to register your work with the U.S. Copyright Office, as the government upholds the rights of such individuals to the fullest extinct of the law.

When Is My Work Protected?
Copyright law affirms "Your work is legally protected the moment it is created and fixed in a tangible form that it is perceptible either directly or with the aid of a machine or device," as noted by the U.S. Copyright Office.

How Long Does A Copyright Last?
Works created after January 1, 1978, lasts the life time of the author, plus 70 years.

What Are The Benefits of Registering My Work With The U.S. Copyright Office?
Registering your work with the United States Copyright Office is strictly voluntary. However, there are major benefits in registering your work as intellectual property. For instance,

- Your work becomes public record.

- As a registered work, you are eligible to claim statutory damages and attorney's fees in litigation, if a legal situation arises.

- Copyright law affirms, "If registration occurs within 5 years of publication, it is considered *prima facie* evidence in a court of law.

See Circular 1, Copyright Basics, section "Copyright Registration" and Circular 38b, Highlights of Copyright Amendments Contained in the Uruguay Round Agreements Act (URAA), on non-U.S. works."

How Much Does It Cost To Register My Work With The U.S. Copyright Office?

Yes, there is a fee to register your work with the U.S. Copyright Office. The U.S. Copyright Office charges $35 to file a Copyright application online and charges $50 to file an application by mail. To learn more about registering your work with the U.S. Copyright Office, please visit http://www.copyright.gov/register, or view basic fees at http://www.copyright.gov.

What Is A Poor Man's Copyright?

A Poor Man's Copyright "refers to the method of using registered dating by the postal service, a notary public or other highly trusted source to date intellectual property, thereby helping to establish that the material has been in one's possession since a particular time, " as defined by Wikipedia The Online Encyclopedia. "The concept is based on the notion that, in the event that such intellectual property were to be misused by a third party, the poor man's copyright would at least establish a legally-recognized date of possession before any proof which a third party may possess.

Is A Poor Man's Copyright Protected By Law?

It is rumored that A Poor Man's Copyright may not always hold up in court. "In countries with no central copyright registration authority, it can be difficult for an author to prove when his or her work was created," according to Wikipedia The Online Encyclopedia. Therefore, in my opinion, A Poor Man's Copyright might lend you some credibility in the courts.

How Can I Create A Poor Man's Copyright?

*Place your created work in an envelope and seal it.

* Place a stamp on the envelope and then, mail it to yourself.

Do not open the envelope when it is returned to you. Keep the package stored away, until you need to show proof that you are the original author of the work, as the United States Post Office stamps a date on the front of the envelope, which establishes a legal date that the package was received by the U.S. Postal service.

How Can I Protect My Intellectual Property Abroad?
"Our international trade agreements and related intellectual property treaties require member countries to provide the means for U.S. rights holders to obtain and enforce intellectual property rights. Intellectual property rights are generally territorial, which means a U.S. patent or trademark provides protection only in the United States," as noted by the U.S. Department of Commerce.

The U.S. Department of Commerce advises owners of intellectual property to go beyond U.S. borders and "register patents and trademarks with the appropriate authorities in each country, or through international treaties that are administered by the World Intellectual Property Organization ." To learn more about intellectual property rights, or to prevent theft and duplications from occurring, please visit the U.S. Department of Commerce at www.StopFakes.gov.

An Important Note
One should consider registering his or her creative works as, "All Rights Reserved." To learn more about protecting your creative works outside the United States, please visit http://www.copyright.gov/circs/circ38a.pdf .

How Can I Apply For A Patent Through The Traditional Patent Process?
Prior to filing a patent application, you must conduct a patent search. Second, prior to filing an application, you must submit the specifications of your work, vow that you are the original creator of the work and third, include any patent application fees along with your application.

What Is A Provisional Application For Patent?
The Provisional Application for Patent is a national application for patent, which offers first-time patent filers a fast and cost-effective way to process

a patent application in the United States. Also, "The Provisional Application for Patent offers applicants parity with foreign applicants under the General Agreement on Tariffs and Trades Uruguay Round Agreements (GATT)," as noted by the U.S. Patent and Trademark Office. To learn more about the (GATT) Uruguay Agreement, please visit http://www.ciesin.org/TG/PI/TRADE/gatt.html or http://www.wto.org/english/thewto_e/whatis_e/tif_e/fact5_e.htm.

How Does The Patent And Trademark Process Work?
"It allows applicants to file a patent without a formal patent claim, oath or declaration or any information disclosure (prior art) statement," as noted by the U.S. Patent and Trademark Office. Second, you can request a Provisional Application for Patent application through the United States Patent and Trademark Office at http://www.uspto.gov/web/forms/index.xml or at http://www.uspto.gov/patents/resources/types/provapp.jsp.

What Are The Benefits of Filing A Provisional Application for Patent?
*It allows you to establish an early effective filing date, with an option to file a non-provisional patent application later.
*It allows the words **'Patent Pending'** to be applied with the description of the invention. However, a Provisional Application for Patent is not available for those filing a design invention.
*It allows immediate commercial promotion of the invention and also, it provides security that helps guard against having your invention stolen.
*In addition, "It allows an option to file multiple provisional applications for patent, with provision to consolidate them in a single non-provisional application for patent," as noted by the U.S. Patent and Trademark Office.

An Important Note
"A Provisional Application for Patent automatically becomes abandoned when its pendency period expires 12 months after the provisional application filing date," as noted by the U.S. Patent and Trademark Office. Therefore, applicants must claim benefit of the patent before it expires. For more information on filing a Provisional Application for Patent, please

visit www.uspto.gov/webforms/index.htm or call 571-272-8800 to talk to the Office of the Deputy Commissioner for Patent Examination Policy.

What Information Is Needed To File A Provisional Application For Patent?

*List the name (s) of inventor(s), and the inventor(s) address.

*List the title of the invention, the registration number of the attorney or agent, if applicable, and list a corresponding address. Also, list any U.S. government agency that might have property interest in the application, along with any required filing fees.

* In addition, inventors must provide a written description of their creations and drawings, to be in compliance with invention codes and the submission process of the application.

How Can I Apply For A Trademark?

First, you must decide what type of intellectual property you need to register. **Second**, familiarize yourself with the basic rules and requirements in filing a trademark registration.

Third, you should conduct a U.S. Patent and Trademark search by searching the U.S. Trademark Electronic Search System, prior to filing an application. Searching the database allows you to see whether someone else has claimed ownership of the mark or whether anyone else has registered the mark with the U.S. Patent and Trademark Office. The search is free via the Internet at http://tess2.uspto.gov.

As a final step, you need to specify goods and services.

Meaning, after you have chosen a mark, you must provide a description of goods and services, and explain how you plan to use the mark in the marketplace.   In short, every application must include a clear representation of the mark.

There are two formats available:

 (1) standard character format,   (2) stylized or a design format

An Important Note

If your mark accompanies a design you must perform a search by using a design code. Please view the **Design Search Code Manual at http://tess2.uspto.gov/tmdb/dscm/index.htm**. For More Information about

Patents And Trademarks, please call the **Trademark Assistance Center** at 1-800-786-9199 and request the *Basic Facts* brochure or paper form.

What Are The Patent And Trademark Response Times?

You can monitor the progress of your application through the **TARR database** at http://tarr.uspto.gov. For more information about trademark registration, please visit http://www.uspto.gov/trademarks/basics/index.jsp.

Sources

U.S. Patent and Trademark Office

 http://www.uspto.gov.

USPTO website

 http://www.uspto.gov/web/patents/pph_index.html.

The Prosecution Highway Program (PPH)

http://www.uspto.gov/patents/init_events/pph/pph_jpo.jsp.

Library of Congress

 http://www.loc.gov/index.html.

Free Merriam Webster Dictionary

http://www.merriam-webster.com/dictionary/copyright

Wikipedia The Online Encyclopedia

http://en.wikipedia.org/wiki/Main_Page.

"You can kill a man but you can't kill an idea."

-Medgar W. Evers-

Photo: Public Domain - Medgar W. Evers (Civil Rights Leader) 1925-1963

Chapter Two

Armed To The Teeth

(A term coined by <u>Tommy Walter</u> on June 7, 2005 at Universal Record/Swollen Member)

This chapter covers the following topics:

Paperwork And Tools Needed To Start A Business

*How To Register A Business With The Federal Government

*Introduction To A Capitalistic Society

*Fico Score And Your Credit Rating

*A List Of Funding Sources

A Proprietor Business

How Can I Apply For An Employer Identification Number?

You can apply for an Employer Identification Number with the Internal Revenue Service. Applicants can call the Business & Specialty Tax line at 1- 800- 829-493. For more information, please visit the IRS at <u>http://www.irs.gov/businesses/small/article/0,,id=97860,00.html</u>.

How Can I Incorporate My Business?

You can register your business as a corporation by state by visiting the FindLaw website at <u>http://smallbusiness.findlaw.com/business-structures/business-structures-resources/business-structures-articles-incorporation.html</u>.

Why Should I Incorporate My Business?

By incorporating, your business assets are set apart from your personal assets. Therefore, if your company is ever sued, your personal assets are not at risk of being taken, as a result of a lawsuit.

How Can I Apply For A Business License?

You must determine what state license or permit you need in order to create your business. Second, check with your local City Hall to see whether any additional licenses or permits are needed to start your business.

What Type Of Bank Account Should I Open For My Business?
You should consider banks that insure your deposits, such as The Federal Deposit Insurance Corporation (FDIC), which is a bank that insures deposits up to $250,000 for fraud and theft.

Why Should I Register My Company With The U.S. Chamber of Commerce?
You should consider registering your company with the U.S. Chamber of Commerce, because your company can receive nationwide exposure. Also, the U.S. Chamber of Commerce can provide you a wealth of knowledge about resources and opportunities that can help you better establish your business. For additional information, please visit the U.S. Chamber of Commerce's website at http://library.uschamber.com.

Why Should I Register My Business With The Better Business Bureau?
The Better Business sets a standard for good business ethics and business practices and therefore, when a company is accredited by the Better Business Bureau, to the world its like receiving a stamp of approval to do business with you. For more information and to register your business with the Better Business Bureau, please visit http://www.bbb.org/us/Business-Accreditation.

What Do I Need To Start A Business?

A Cash Register	A Receipt Book
A Computer	A Feasible Marketing Strategy
A Printer	A Telephone
A registered business address (P.O. Box)	Bookkeeping Software/Flyers
A Fax Machine	Invoices and Order Purchases

How Can I Start A Nonprofit Organization?
The basic paperwork needed
*Specify the organization's purpose and function
*Draft bylaws, which are the governing documents of the organization. Bylaws explain how the organization operates; its intent and purpose.

What Is The Process In Setting Up A Nonprofit Organization?
*First, you will need to apply for an Employer Identification Number by calling the IRS at 1-800-829-4933, or you can download Form SS-4 at http://www.irs.gov/businesses/small/article/0,,id=102767,00.html .
*Second, draft the organization's By-laws
*Third, apply for Articles of Incorporation (This step is optional. You do not have to incorporate your organization). However, if you desire to incorporate, you can apply for Articles of Incorporation with your local Secretary of State office for a small fee.
*Fourth, you can apply for a 501 C-3 nonprofit tax-exempt status by contacting the IRS at 1-877-829-5500, or visit the IRS at http://www.irs.gov/charities/charities to download an application.
*Fifth, apply for liability and employee health insurance coverage.
*Sixth, open a business checking account with a (FDIC) Bank.
* Last (optional), register your organization with the U.S. Chamber of Commerce where consumers are able to verify the company as reputable.

Who Should Oversee The Board?
*You can elect or appoint the executive board, which oversees the entire operations of the organization. However, it is wise to keep board members at an odd-number in order to avoid a tie at election time, or when voting on other business matters on behalf of the organization.
*Executive board members are needed to ensure the organization is operating within the guidelines of its established bylaws.
Determine who will lead your board. Generally, this person is the founder of the organization. By appointing the founder as the C.E.O. and overseer of the board, allows him or her to maintain control of the organization, as well as ensure the company's intent and purpose. Further, you will need a Vice-President, a treasurer, a secretary, a public relations person, and an attorney. An attorney can draft legal documents on behalf of the organization, view insurance policies, as well as help prevent lawsuits from occurring.
Think Smart! Your organization's success is weighed heavily upon choosing the right board members. One should consider selecting prominent and influential persons, those who are knowledgeable in

serving on boards, including those who are accessible to federal and state funding, or those who are knowledgeable about other forms of philanthropy. **Who are these people?** They are your judges, accountants, bankers, teachers, lawyers, community leaders, government workers, and politicians, as they can gain access to valuable information about grants and their availability. **Last,** keep in mind your company is new and lacks reputation and self-sufficiency, so choosing key players to help establish your organization's stability is paramount.

Who Should I Select To Run Daily Operations?
*A Chief Executive Officer (C.E.O.)
*A Vice-President
*An Accountant/Bookkeeper
*A Secretary
*A Public Relations Person
*Lay people-those who perform daily tasks and operations.

A List Of Funding Sources And Consulting Programs That Can Help You Establish Your Business

Small Business Administration
www.sba.gov

Black Women Enterprises
www.blackwomenenterprises.org

Latino Business Women
www.hermana.org

National Association of Women Business Owners
www.nawbo.org

Online Government Grant Application
Billions of dollars are available for small business, Education, Housing, Minority and Women Government Grants at http://www.ineedgrants.com,

or at http://www.AmericaGovernmentGrants.com.

P2P Lending Marketplace For Personal & Small Business Loans
http://www.Prosper.com

Small Business Association
www.sba.org
http://www.sba.gov/smallbusinessplanner/start/financestartup/index.html,
or visit www.sba.gov/aboutsba/sbaprograms/**sbdc**/index.html for
entrepreneurs.

S.C.O.R.E. (Small Business Mentoring and Training Organization) at
www.score.org, or visit S.C.O.R.E at
http://www.score.org/template_gallery.html.

Introduction To A Capitalistic Society

First, how can we discuss money without mentioning capitalism, the U.S.
Federal Reserves, and taxes. If you plan to acquire wealth in America,
you must first, understand how wealth is generated in a capitalistic society.

What Is Capitalism?
Capitalism is "a way of organizing an economy so things that are used to
make and transport products (such as land, oil, factories, ships, etc.), are
owned by individual people and companies rather than the government,"
as defined by Merriam-Webster dictionary.

How Is Communism And Socialism Different From Capitalism?
Communism is a system, in which the government owns everything, and
the citizens are denied the right to even own property.

Socialism is a system, in which industries are either owned, or controlled
by the government, instead of by individuals or companies.
Now, I ask you, "What system allows its citizens the best passageway to
accumulate wealth?" I know for me, it is the capitalistic society, which I
am delighted to take part.

What Is The Federal Reserve?

The Federal Reserve was created in 1913. The Federal Reserve sets the nation's monetary policy and interest rates, it regulates banking institutions, and provides financial services to the government. Currently, there are twelve regional Federal Reserve Banks in America. In short, The Federal Reserve is the central banking system of the United States.

What Should I Know About Taxes?

The most important thing to understand about taxes in America is to understand that you have to pay them. If you do not pay your taxes, you can be fined and arrested.

Briefly, the United States tax system includes federal, state, local and county governments. As for federal taxes, in which the Internal Revenue oversees, "The federal government collects several specified taxes, in addition to the general income tax, such as Social Security and Medicare, which are large social support programs that are funded by taxes on personal earned income. Estate taxes are levied on inheritance. Net long-term capital gains, as well as certain types of qualified dividend income are taxed preferentially. Also, federal excise taxes are applied to specific items such as motor fuels, tires, telephone usage, tobacco products, and alcoholic beverages. Excise taxes are often, but not always, allocated to special funds related to the object or activity taxed," as defined by the United States Department of Treasury, and Wikipedia The Online Encyclopedia.

How Does The Credit System In America Work?

Americans are approved or disapproved credit through a process known as the Fico Score System, which was first introduced by the Fair, Isaac and Company founded in 1956. Creditors measure consumers' credit worthiness using a point system based on a scale from 300 – 850 points; 300 being the lowest possible score and 850 being the maximum score available.

How Is My Fico Score Measured?

*A person's credit history makes up 35 percent of the FICO Score rating.
*A person's income to debt ratio makes up 30 percent of the FICO score.
*The length of a person's credit history makes up 15 percent of the FICO Score. Therefore, it is not good to have accounts in good standing deleted from your credit record. If a good account has been deleted from your

credit record, you can submit a letter to the credit bureau to have it re-added to your credit history, as it will help you improve your FICO Score.
*New accounts make up 10 percent of a person's FICO score. Therefore, if you apply for frequent lines of credit, your credit score would decrease.
*The type of credit a person has makes up 10 percent of the Fico Score. Therefore, making a major purchase, such as buying a car, a home or having revolving credit can improve your Fico Score rating.

What Is Considered A Good Credit Rating/Score?

A good credit score is at least 720 or higher, according to The Fair Isaac Corporation guidelines. However, some creditors consider 650 or higher as a good credit rating. In short, having a good credit rating allow consumers to open new lines of credit at lower interest rates; the lower your credit rating, the higher interest you pay on lines of credit.

How Can I Make My Credit Bad?

*Delinquency
*Not paying an account in- full
*Credit to debt income ratio is too high
*Applying for frequent lines of credit
*Car repossession
*Overall debt, if too much, can cause poor credit.
*Co-signing for someone else who cannot
pay a debt and you cannot afford to make payments on their behalf.
*Charge-offs
*Foreclosures
*Tax Liens
*Bankruptcy (the worst case scenario)
To learn more, please visit FDIC at
http://www.fdic.gov/deposit/insurance/risk/assesrte.html, or view
Improving Your Fico Credit Score at
http://www.myfico.com/CreditEducation/ImproveYourSCore.aspx.

Sources

FDIC at http://www.fdic.gov/deposit/deposits/insured/index.html.
US Department of Treasury at
http://treas.tpaq.treasury.gov/topics/taxes/index.shtml or
http://treas.tpaq.treasury.gov/offices/tax-policy.
Small Business Mentoring and Training organization (S.C.O.R.E)

U.S. Chamber of Commerce at http://www.uschamber.com
The Internal Revenue Service
Merriam-Webster Dictionary
Wikipedia The Free Encyclopedia at
http://en.wikipedia.org/wiki/Taxation_in_the_United_States.

"Delay is preferable to error"
-Thomas Jefferson-

Photo: Public Domain - A photo of Thomas Jefferson by <u>Gilbert Stuart</u>, <u>1805</u>.

Chapter Three
DREAM BIG
(Donald J. Trunp uses this term often)

This chapter covers the following topic:
Easy And Affordable Ways To Start A Business
1. Start A Shoe Shine Business or Accessory Store
2. Start A Book Vendor
3. Start A Food Vendor
4. Start A Home-Based Business
5. Start A Consulting Business
6. Start A Sewing and Alterations Shop
7. Start A Shoe Repair Business
8. Start A Computer Repair Business
9. Start A Home-Based Day Care Center
10. Start A Home-Based Catering Business
11. Start A Carpet and Upholstery Business
12. Start A Plumbing Company with tools, a truck, and license
13. Start A Landscaping Business
14. Start A Window Cleaning Business (Contract with companies)
15. Start An Online Business
16. Start A Scrap Medal Business/Haul scrap medal to the junk yard
17. Start Renting Your Property to Others (Become A Landlord)
18. Start A Home-Based Self-Publishing Business
19. Start A Consulting Business
20. Start A Home-Based Record or Production Company
21. Start A Home-Based Video Production Company
22. Start A Mary Kay Business
23. Start A Moving Furniture Business
24. Start A Pet Grooming Business
25. Start An Online Referral Service
26. Start A Fitness Program (Become a consultant or trainer)
27. Start A Notary Republic Business (Become A Notary)
28. Start A Home-Based Accounting and Tax Service Business

29. Start An Interior or Exterior Painting Company
30. Start An Underground Water Sprinkler Company
31. Start A Home –Based Foster Care Business
32. Start A Home for the Aging
33. Start A Locksmith Business
34. Start A Cooking and Tutoring Service Business
35. Start A Wedding or Party Planner Business
36. Start A DJ or Party Consultant Business
37. Start A Barber Shop
38. Start A Beauty Shop
39. Start A Photography or Graphics Design Business
40. Start A Fitness or Weight Training Business
41. Start A Floor and Tile Business
42. Start A Repair Shop (computers, electronics, or televisions)

An Important Note

Businesses listed above might need additional licensing. Please contact your local County Clerk's Office to see whether any additional licenses are needed in order to start your business. Second, always have a business plan on-hand, because you never know who may want to invest in you . If you are interested in writing a professional business plan, you can contact "S.C.O.R.E." at http://www.score.org/template_gallery.html.

Chapter Four
WHO SAID YOU CAN'T GET SOMETHING FOR NOTHING
(Neil Peart quotes Canadian Drummer for the band Rush b.1952)

This chapter covers the following topic:

TWENTY-FIVE BUSINESS FREEBIES THAT CAN HELP YOU ESTABLISH YOUR BUSINESS

Starting a business has never been easier, if you know where to catch a break. In this chapter, you will discover many websites that can assist you in developing your business, as they offer free services, and free business items. Please visit the websites below and save BIG!

The websites below offer the following services:

1. https://secure2.web.com/cart/domain.aspx
   *Request a free online store, domain, or a free website for your business.

2. http://www.free-press-release.com
   *Request a free press release and business promotions.

3. http://www.shippingsidekick.com
   *Request free goods for eBay businesses or small business ventures
   *Request tracking services for packages through U.S.P.S, DHL, FedEx, and UPS.
   *Compare shipping rates, company moving rates, car and truck shipping rates, and etc.

4. http://www.vstore.ca
   *Request free ecommerce solutions, and free sub-domains.
   *Request a free shopping cart or free V-store.
   *Request a free ecommerce website or free web host.

5. http://www.1freecart.com
   *Request a free online cart store: shopping cart software,

* PayPal, MySpace, or e-Commerce shopping cart.

6. http://www.all-free-isp.com
   *Request free Internet access.

7. http://www.dialupforfree.com/(DialUpForFree
   *Request free dial up Internet service for Windows and
   Mac computers in the United States

8. http://www.cdotfree.com
   *Request free dial up Internet service in Canada.

9. http://www.free-dial.co.uk
   *Request free dial up Internet service in the United Kingdom.
   *Request free support for Mac and Windows operating systems.

10. http://www.eblogus.com/start.php
    *Request a free Blog.

11. http://microbloghost.com
    *Request a free Twitter-like micro-blog.

12. http://www.tornadostream.com
    *Request a free online radio station or music library.

13. http://theblogs.net
    *Request a free Blog.
    *Request free publishing for your diaries, journals, and articles.

14. http://www.thefreesite.com/Mobile_Phone_Freebies
    *Request free ring tone downloads for your cell phone.

15. http://www.vistaprint.com/free-business-
    cards.aspx?GP=7%2f1%2f2010+2%3a40%3a37+PM.
    *Request free business cards and templates.

16. www.freebusinesscards.com/ or http://www.freebusinesscards.com
    *Request free business cards.

17. http://www.freeprintablebusinesscards.net
     *Request free printable business cards.

18. http://www.inflowinventory.com
    *Request a free InFlow Software Inventory System.
    *Request a free tracking system for customer returns, invoices, orders, and to process payments.

19. http://www.idontpay.com/smallbusiness.html
    *Request free business samples and printing services.

20. http://www.unionpen.com/Default.aspx?FocusId=samples.htm
    *Request free office supplies and/or business supply samples.

21. **IRS FREE File**
    http://www.irs.gov/efile/article/0,,id=118986,00.html
    *Request free federal income tax preparation and electronic filing for eligible taxpayers.

22. http://quickbooks.intuit.com/qb/products/common/direct_download/email.jsp
    *Request free accounting software download s for Intuit QuickBooks and Software for Windows.
    *Request free tracking up to 20 customers for small businesses.

23. http://www.pbooks.org/blog
    *Request free bookkeeping software.

24. http://www.freebyte.com/free_computers/#freecomputers
    *Request a free computer

25. http://www.presentationmagazine.com/free-powerpoint-download-51.html
    *Request free PowerPoint download and free phone activation service.

Money Savings Nugget

To save on telephone expenses, you can register your business with Google Voice online number. You can make and receive calls straight from your laptop or any basic computer, all you need to do is create an account through Google Voice at https://www.google.com/accounts/ServiceLogin?service=grandcentral&passive=1209600&continue=https://www.google.com/voice&followup=https://www.google.com/voice&ltmpl=open. It's free for the U.S. and Canada.

"Those who know, do and those who understand, teach."

-Aristole-

Photo: **Public Domain** - **Aristotle Pictures - Aristotle from The School of Athens**
With gratitude to School Mathematics/Statistics University of St Andrews, Scotland

Chapter Five
A PENNY SAVED IS A PENNY EARNED
(By Benjamin Franklin)

This chapter covers the following topic:
FTC's Way To Save You Money
According to the Federal Trade Commission, there are sixty-six ways consumers can save, and get more for their money.

How Can I Save On Airfare?
1. FTC says the best deals for airfare may not be available in your local area, but might be available through major carriers that fly to your destination.
2. FTC advises us to purchase tickets at least 14 days in advance or include a Saturday evening stay-over with our trip. By doing this, it is believed that we can book a flight at a lower rate.
3. FTC says we should consider checking fare rates online to search for discounted prices, even if we have the assistance of a travel agent.

How Can I Save On Car Rentals?
4. FTC says we should take advantage of special offers and membership discounts.
5. FTC says we should consider car rentals that offer various insurance and waiver options.

How Can I Save When Purchasing A New Car?
6. FTC says shop smart! Meaning, choose a car model that is lower in price, along with having low depreciation, finance, insurance, gasoline, maintenance and repair costs. FTC claims we can save thousands of dollars over a life by doing this.
7. FTC says we can save hundreds of dollars through comparison shopping. FTC says, simply shop around and compare quotes from various dealers before we give into the first offer that comes our way.
8. FTC says, once we sign a contract, the car is legally ours. So, shop

around consumers and be anxious for nothing, I say. In all that we do, we must make sure to do our homework before purchasing a car.

How Can I Save When Purchasing A Used Car?

9. Before we buy, FTC says we should search the bluebook price for the actual value of the car. Once we have done this, FTC says we are now ready to compare the actual value of the car to the dealer's asking price. FTC says we should have our cars inspected by a trusted or licensed mechanic, especially if we are buying a car **"SOLD- AS- IS!"**

10. FTC says, if we are considering purchasing a used car, we should consider purchasing it from someone that we know. FTC claims by doing this, we will probably receive a lower offer than we would if we bought a car from a retail seller. Also, FTC says we might gain invaluable insight about the car's history.

How Can I Save When Leasing A Car?

11. FTC says leasing payments are usually lower than the average car loan payment, but FTC still advises us not to base our decision solely on this notion, when considering to buy a leased vehicle.

12. FTC says payments are usually lower for leased vehicles, because we do not own the car. FTC says, as we shop for a leased vehicle, we should take into consideration the capitalized price of the vehicle. In other words, FTC says we should take into account the actual price of the car, including trade-in options, the down payment amount, the monthly payment, and other fees that might be included in the price of the vehicle.

FTC says a valuable source to consider prior to purchasing a leased vehicle is the Consumer Services Guide, which is a directory, in which the Federal Reserve Board offers at http://www.consumerservicesguide.org.

How Can I Save When Purchasing Gasoline?

13. FTC says we should compare prices at various gasoline stations; choose a self-serve gas station, instead of a full-service gas station. FTC says by choosing a low-cost octane, instead of the higher cost- octane, we can save hundreds of dollars a year.

14. FTC says we should keep our car engine tuned up, as well as keep our tires at the right pressure points. By doing this, FTC claimed we can save up to $100 a year.

How Can I Save On Car Repairs?

15. FTC says consumers lose billions of dollars on unnecessary car repairs. FTC says find an honest and skilled mechanic to do the work on our cars.
*Choose a mechanic that is certified or established.
*Choose a mechanic that communicates clearly the repairs needed and the costs before we let someone repair the vehicle.

How Can I Save On Auto Insurance?

16. FTC says we should consider purchasing insurance from a low- price, licensed insurance dealer. FTC says we can save several hundred dollars a year by doing this. Also, FTC says we can call the state insurance department for a price list to learn the basic insurance rates of various insurance companies. FTC advises us to call at least four (4) companies that offer the lowest insurance rates, and then see which one will offer us the best deal in terms of cost.

17. FTC says we can lower our insurance payments, if we have an older car. Also, FTC says we can drop collision and comprehensive coverage, which can save us money and generate lower monthly insurance payments. FTC says we can save hundreds of dollars on insurance premiums by doing this.

18. FTC says we should make sure that the new insurance policy is activated before we drop the old insurance policy.

How Can I Save On My Homeowners or Renters Insurance?

19. Purchase insurance from a low-price licensed insurer. FTC says we can save several hundred dollars a year on our homeowner insurance, including renter's insurance up to $50 a year.
*FTC says we can request a publication that discloses the basic costs for insurance by contacting our local state insurance department.

20. FTC says we should make sure that we purchase enough insurance to cover the value of our home. In other words, we should maintain enough coverage on our home to rebuild it, in case our home is declared a total loss. **21.** FTC says we should make sure that the new insurance policy is in full effect prior to cancelling our old insurance policy.

How Can I Save On Life Insurance?

22. Although Term Life Insurance does not offer investments or savings options, FTC says Term Life is the cheapest way to go, if we are only needing basic coverage.

23. If we purchase Whole Life Insurance, Universal Life or etc., FTC says we should plan to have it fifteen years. By canceling the policy sooner, FTC says this could double our insurance costs.

24. FTC says we should always reference the National Association of Insurance Commissioners or library in order to research an insurance company's background or financial standing. Please visit the (NAIC) at http://www.naic.org.

How Can I Save Money When Banking?
Checking Accounts and Debit Cards

25. FTC says by choosing a free checking account, we can save more than $100 a year in annual fees. Also, FTC says the same is true when selecting a checking account that has no balance requirements.

26. FTC says we should beware of AMT charges associated with financial institutions prior to choosing a bank.

How Can I Save On Bank Products?

27. FTC says we should consider having our accounts insured by FDIC or NCUA credit unions, prior to opening a savings account.

28. FTC says we should compare rates and fees of other financial institutions.

29. FTC advises us to shop around for the highest return on savings accounts. FTC says when we are looking to invest, we should consider investing in CDs or U.S. Savings Bond Series I or EE, which have little or no risk.

How Can I Save When Using My Credit Card?

30. FTC says we should send payments in seven to 10 days earlier than when our payment is due. FTC says, by doing this, we can avoid late fees or increased interest rates. Also, FTC says late payments on one credit card can cause interest rates to increase on all the other credit cards that we have in our possession, as well.

31. FTC says we can avoid interest charges completely if we are willing to pay off our charges at the end of each month. FTC says we should try to shift the remaining balance of the card to another card that has a lower APR.

32. FTC says that we should beware of credit cards that offer cash back, travel awards, rebates or other perks, because they may require us to pay higher fees and rates.

How Can I Save On An Auto Loan?

33. FTC says we can save several thousand dollars in finance charges by paying cash for a vehicle. FTC claims, by making a large down payment or shopping for the shortest term loan and/or finding a lower interest rate loan, we can save lots of money in the long run.

34. FTC says we can save $1,000 in finance charges by shopping for the cheapest loan, getting a rate quote, or preapproved loan from a bank or credit union. FTC says financing a car through the dealership will cost us more.

35. FTC says acquiring a zero or low-rate financing loan from the dealer may stop us from receiving a rebate. FTC encourages us to become familiar with the terms low-rate financing and lower sale price, so we can understand them and also, be able to understand the differences between them.

How Can I Save On My First Mortgage Loan?

36. If our monthly mortgage payments are high, FTC says we can still save tens of thousands of dollars in interests' fees by getting a short-term mortgage, but one, in which we you can still afford.

37. FTC says we can save thousands of dollars in interest fees by obtaining a low-rate mortgage, which offers the fewest points.

38. FTC says we can surf the Internet for mortgage rate surveys and afterwards, call lenders about the rates, and possibly negotiate a better price.

39. FTC says we need to understand that the adjustable rate mortgage can vary significantly over the lifetime of the loan, FTC advises us to ask lenders about the highest rate that we would have to pay on any given loan.

40. Also, FTC says consumers might consider refinancing their mortgages in order to lower mortgage rates.

How Can I Save Money When Applying For A Home Equity Loan?

41. FTC says that we need to be cautious when taking out a home equity loan. FTC says loans may eliminate the equity in our homes.
If we cannot pay our loan, FTC says we stand a good chance of losing our home.

42. FTC says we need to compare prices and shop around for the best home equity loan. FTC says we should consider the interest rate on the loan, origination fees, discount points, and etc. Also, FTC says we need to ask about rate changes.

How Can I Save When Searching For Rental Property?

43. FTC says we should try to negotiate a lower sales price by hiring a broker, and ask to view any properties that have already been listed.

44. FTC says we should not purchase a home until it has been inspected by a home inspector.

45. FTC says, in addition to searching for homes through the classifieds, referrals, and/or asking friends about renting, we can also contact the building manager or owner where we desire to live.

46. FTC says signing a lease obligates us to monthly payments, which should be outlined in the agreement.

How Can I Save On Home Improvement Projects?

47. FTC says home improvement projects can costs thousands of dollars, and can leave homeowners filing a lot of complaints, if the work is not done satisfactory. FTC advises us to choose an established, licensed contractor who submits repair costs in writing.

48. Also, FTC advises us not to pay contractors the total amount for repairs upfront. In fact, FTC advises us to sign the contract only after the work has been done to our satisfaction.

How Can I Save When Purchasing Major Appliances?

49. FTC advises us to research consumer reports prior to buying a major appliance. FTC says we should reference a public library about appliances, the brand names, as well as learn how to evaluate appliances that we are interested in buying.

*In addition, FTC advises us to search the Yellow Energy Guide about potential products. To learn more, please visit http://www.energystar.gov/index.cfm?c=appliances.pr_energy_guide.

*FTC says choosing an appliance that has earned the government's "ENERGY STAR," can save us up to 50% in energy usage.

50. After choosing a specific model, FTC advises us to search the yellow pages or the Internet to locate stores that carry the brand of merchandise that we are interested in buying. Also, FTC says it would not hurt us to do some comparison shopping, which can also save us up to $100 on the best bargains.

How Can I Save On Heating And Cooling Bills?

51. FTC says having an energy audit can save us up to hundreds of dollars a yea, such as in air conditioning unit and heating units.

FTC says we can request an audit from the electric or gas company at anytime. However, in some cases, we might be required to pay a service fee. Also, if the utility company cannot perform the service, FTC says we can ask the representatives if they are aware of anyone who can provide the service for us.

52. FTC says we can save up to $100 a year in electricity costs by enrolling in the Cost-Savings Program, such as the

*Load Management Program, or the

*Off-Hour Rate Program that is offered through the electric company. Also, FTC says we can contact our local electric company and inquire about the programs.

How Can I Save On My Utility Bills?
Telephone Service

53. FTC advises us to review our service terms once a year, and to check and see what wireless and cable companies are charging for the services that we are not currently using. FTC says we should consider comparison shopping to find the cheapest plan that is available to us, as well as one that meets our needs. Also, FTC says that we should consider buying a packaged deal or (a bundled package) that offer us various services such as, local toll, long distance, and other desired services that can be cost-effective.

54. Also, FTC recommends that we evaluate our existing plan to determine what features we are not using. According to FTC, "Each plan dropped could save us $40 or more each year."

55. FTC says if we rarely use the services provided, we should consider dropping the plan altogether or avoid plans that charge monthly fees for minimums. FTC says we should consider using "dial around services, such as 10-40 numbers or prepaid phone cards for our calls."

An Important Note

FTC says when using services, such as dial around, we should beware of f minimum fees, and per minute rates. Also, FTC says we need to investigate whether the cards have an expiration date.

56. FTC says when using a cell phone, we need to make sure that we choose an adequate plan that meets your needs. FTC says we should consider peak calling periods, area coverage, roaming charges, and termination costs.

57. FTC says we should compare per minute rates and surcharges on cell phones, prepaid phone cards, and etc., before making calls away from home.

58. FTC recommends that we make long distance calls directly. In other words, avoid using operator assistance when placing a call. FTC says placing an operated- assistance call can cost us up to $10 extra. Also, FTC says before we contact the operator for assistance, we should first, consider surfing the Internet or telephone directory.

How Can I Save On Other Things, such as Purchasing Food In Supermarkets?

59. FTC says we can shop at lower-priced food stores to save money. FTC says convenient stores have been known to charge higher prices.

60. FTC says we should purchase only the things that we need and that we can do this easily by sticking to our grocery list as we shop.

61. FTC claims comparison shopping on unit prices, shelf labels, and price-per-ounce items can save consumers hundreds of dollars a year.

How Can I Save On Prescription Drugs?

62. FTC says buying generic drugs, instead of name brand drugs can save us money.

63. FTC advises us to call several pharmacies to see which one has the cheaper prices. Also, FTC says we should consider mail-order pharmacies, which can prove less expensive in purchasing prescription drugs.

How Can I Save On Funeral Expenses?

64. FTC says we can save money by planning ahead and by preparing for our burial arrangements and memorial services before we die.

65. FTC advises us to contact the Funeral Consumer Alliance or Memorial Society to find out the most affordable way to burry a love one. FTC says by doing this, we can save several thousand dollars.

66. FTC advises us to call various funeral homes and inquire about the costs of goods and services, in which they offer, instead of choosing a funeral service blindly. By law, FTC says we are entitled to an itemized list of charges prior to contracting with any funeral home that whishes to render us services.

Upside Down Loans And How To Avoid Them

What Is An Upside Down Loan?

The term usually refers to a car loan, in which the loan amount is more than the value of the car. In short, it is a loan that has a negative equity.

How Does An Upside Down Loan Occur?

An upside down car loan can occur, as a result of paying too much for a vehicle. In other words, you pay more for the car than what it is actually worth. Also, an upside down loan can occur, if you paid a low down payment on the car, or the loan agreement is for a lengthy time, which has you paying car payments on a vehicle that has depreciated way below market value.

How Can I Avoid An Upside Down Loan?

According bankrate.com, there are nine (9) ways to avoid an upside down car loan:

"*Pay at least 20 percent down on the car at purchase
  *Do not finance taxes or fees
  *Take out the shortest term loan that you can afford.
  *Don't take out a loan for longer than you plan to keep the car
  *Consider Gap Insurance
  *Buy a used car
  * Keep the car until its value matches or exceeds the balance on the loan.
  * Buy cheap
  * Sell your car yourself."

What Is Gap Insurance?

Gap Insurance pays the difference between the cash value of the vehicle and the outstanding balance owed on the car loan or lease. Also, you must purchase gap insurance at the time you purchase your car. However, when sell or trade your vehicle before it is paid off, you should receive a partial refund from your gap insurance.

Where Can I Purchase Gap Insurance?

You can purchase Gap Insurance at your local insurance company, or from a national insurance company. Please visit *www.quicken.com/insurance*, or *www.insweb.com* to get insurance quotes.

Sources

The Federal Trade Commission, June 2006 – Last updated April 2009
www.ftc.gov/bcp/edu/pubs/consumer/general/gen14.shtm.
Washington State Office of the Insurance Commissioner
http://www.insurance.wa.gov/consumers/Complaints.shtml.
Consumer Reports at http://www.consumerReports.org, and
Bankrate.com.

"There is only one good, knowledge and one evil, ignorance."

-Socrates-

**Photo Public Domain: Socrates, a Greek (Athenian) Philosopher
469 BC–399 BC[1]**

Chapter Six
A Fool And His Money Will Soon Depart
(By Thomas Tusser 1557)

This chapter covers the following topics:

Businesses And Utilities That May Owe You Money

*How Can I Receive Additional Checks From Social Security?

*How Can I Request Extended Legal Protection Under The Service Members Civil Relief Act of 2003-2004?

*How Can I Request A Check From My Landlord/Rental Office?

*How Can I Request A Check Before I Am Evicted?

*How Can I Request Unemployment Compensation When I Retire?

*How Can I Request A Check From My Private Mortgage Insurance?

*How Can I Request A Check When My Property Has Been Stolen?

*How Can I Request A Check From The Water Company?

*How Can I Request A Check From The Gas Company?

*How Can I Request A Check From The Electric Company?

An Important Note

Under the Federal Trade Commission Act (15 U.S.C. §§ 41-58, <u>as amended</u>), the Federal Trade Commission can "Prevent unfair methods of competition, and unfair or deceptive business acts, or practices in or affecting commerce."

How Can I Receive An Additional Check From Social Security?

According to Social Security guidelines, spouses may be eligible to receive up to 50% of their spouse's Social Security benefits. If your spouse has the highest wages, you might consider claiming his or her Social Security benefits.

How Can I Draw My Spouse's Social Security Benefits?

*You must be at least 62 years of age
*You must wait until your spouse draws his or her own Social Security benefits before you can claim spousal benefits, or
*You can have a qualifying child who is under the age of 16, or a child who is disabled. To learn more, please visit Social Security Administration at <u>www.ssa.gov/OACT/quickcalc/spouse.html</u>.

How Can I Claim My Ex-Spouse's Social Security Benefits?

According to Social Security guidelines, an ex- spouse may be eligible to claim survival benefits if he or she meets the following criteria:

"* Be at least age 60 years old (or 50 if disabled) and have been married to you for at least 10 years; or
* Be any age if he or she is caring for a child who is eligible for benefits based on your earnings; and
* Not be eligible for an equal or higher benefit based on his or her own work; and not be currently married, unless the remarriage occurred after age 60 or after age 50 if disabled," as noted by the Social Security Administration.

How Can I Claim And Suspend My Social Security Benefits?

By claiming and suspending benefit payments, the lower earning spouse can claim spousal benefits, as the higher earning spouse continues to work, earning what is called "**delayed retirement credits**." However, the lower earning spouse cannot claim the higher Social Security benefit, until the higher earning spouse files his or her Social Security claim. In short, claiming and suspending benefit payments has been said to maximize lifetime and survivor benefits. However, the Social Security Administration advises those who choose to delay their retirement benefits to sign up for Medicare at age 65 to avoid being delayed benefits later; or to avoid paying higher cost for Medicare. To learn more, please visit Social Security Administration at http://www.ssa.gov/retire2/delayret.htm; or visit http://www.socialsecurity.gov/retire2/applying8.htm.

How Can I Claim Social Security Benefits Twice?
You can claim benefits twice, if both persons in the marriage worked and have reached full retirement age.
First, you are entitled to claim Social Security benefits based on your own work history and second, you are entitled to claim Social Security as a spouse. To learn more, please visit Social Security Administration at http://www.socialsecurity.gov/pubs/10024.html#yourfamily or http://www.socialsecurity.gov/retire2/applying8.htm.

How Can I Receive Social Security Benefits For My Children?
 "Social Security recipients who have children younger than 18, or between 18 and 19 years old can receive benefits, if they attend elementary or secondary school as full-time students; or children ages 18 or older who are severely disabled can receive benefits. However, the child's disability must have started before age 22 to be eligible, as noted by the Social Security Administration.

An Important Note
Also, the eligible child is entitled to receive monthly benefits up to 50% of the retiree's benefit amount. However, there is a cap on how much a family can receive from Social Security. To learn more, please visit Social Security Administration at http://www.socialsecurity.gov/pubs/10024.html#yourfamily.

How Can I Claim Survivors Benefits?
According to Social Security Administration, a widow or widower who is:
   "*   60 or older
    *   50 or older and disabled, or
    *   Any age if he or she is caring for your child who is younger than 16 or disabled and entitled to Social Security on your record."
Also, your children may be eligible to receive survivor benefits if they are unmarried and are under the age of 18. To learn more please visit

http://www.socialsecurity.gov/pubs/10024.html#yourfamily.   In addition, Social Security pays a one-time payment of $255 to a surviving spouse or child after your death. However, strict guidelines do apply.

How Can I Boost My Social Security Benefits When Filing FORM SSA-521?

Apparently, there are rumors that you can receive an extra $1,000 a month from Social Security by filing FORM SSA-521. According to Olivia Martin, Sr. Researcher, S&A Investment Research, who wrote a brief article about it on October 10, 2008. Personally, I have not researched this claim thoroughly, but I did learn the Social Security Administration offers FORM SSA-521 online at http://www.socialsecurity.gov/online/ssa-521.pdf.

Second, I learned that AARP published an article on June 11, 2008, titled "Paying Back Social Security: Does It Make Sense?" by Karen M. Kroll, which provided information in how to file FORM SSA-521, and how it allegedly works. To learn more about the article, please visit http://www.aarp.org/work/social-security/info-04-2009/paying_back_social.html.

An Important Note

In my opinion, the best way to learn about FORM SSA-521 is contact the Social Security Administration Office and ask questions. You can download FORM SSA-521 at http://www.socialsecurity.gov/online/ssa-521.pdf.

Sources

 AARP at http://assets.aarp.org.

U.S. Social Security Administration at http://www.ssa.gov.

U.S. Department of Labor at http://workforcesecurity.doleta.gov/unemploy/uifactsheet.asp.

The Servicemembers Civil Relief Act of 2003 amended the Sailors Civil Relief Act of 1940.

What Is The Servicemembers Civil Relief Act?

The Act was signed into law under the Bush Administration on December 19, 2004. The Act is intended to protect active duty servicemembers from potential legal problems and extend their civil protection rights.

Second, being prior military, I understand all too well about a solder's responsibility in honoring his or her financial responsibilities. However, when an active duty servicemember, reserve, or National Guard member is called to war or receives orders to serve a remote assignment, I found through personal experience, one's financial obligation can become difficult to manage.

What Benefits Can I Receive From The Servicemembers Civil Relief Act of 2003-2004?
The Act was signed into law on December 13, 2003 by President Bush. The Act is a complete revision of the Soldiers' and Sailors' Civil Relief Act of 1940. However, it was revised again in 2004.
The Act protects servicemembers from being sued, while serving at war or when serving an out of the country tour. The Act can protect servicemembers from foreclosure, eviction, high interest-rate loans, including rates on mortgages, and other debt obligations. In short, the Act provides extended legal protection for servicemen, in which servicemembers have been allowed to postpone or suspend certain civil obligations due to mitigating circumstances. To learn more about additional benefits covered under the Act, please visit http://www.robins.af.mil/shared/media/document/AFD-090317-053.pdf, http://www.federalreserve.gov/boarddocs/supmanual/cch/200911/scra.pdf.

Sources
U.S. Department of Defense
http://www.defense.gov/specials/Relief_Act_Revision
Consumer Compliance Handbook
http://www.federalreserve.gov/boarddocs/supmanual/cch/200911/scra.pdf.

What Is A Security Deposit?
Under the Landlord and Tenant Act, a landlord can request a security deposit from prospective renters, prior to leasing them a unit, space or an apartment. In short, a security deposit works as an incentive to keep rental property in good condition. In short, the law places a mandate on landlords to return a tenant's security deposit, with interest, if no damages have been done to the rental property.

What Happens To My Security Deposit After I Give It To My Landlord?
Under the Landlord and Tenant Act or in some cases, The Rent Security

Deposit Act, landlords/rental offices are required to do the following:
*Place the tenant's security deposit in a separate interest-bearing or escrow bank account, which is federally insured.
*Tell tenants the name and address of the bank where their security deposits are being kept.
*Tell tenants the type of account that has been set-up in their name.
*Tell tenants the current interest rate on the account.
*Usually, landlords must submit this information to you in writing 30 days after the security deposit has been accepted.

How Can I Request My Security Deposit Back With Interest?

Under the Landlord and Tenant Act, landlords are required to return your security deposit within a time period set forth by law, which is usually 30-45 days after the termination of tenancy. Also, a tenant can request an interest check from the landlord or rental office after a period of one year. Below, are the basic steps in requesting an interest check.
***First**, submit your request in writing and make sure you include the law, in which you are basing your request upon.
***Second,** in the letter include your address, apartment number, the date you moved in your apartment, the amount of your security deposit, and the current interest rate that you should receive on the deposit, as well as the expected time frame that you should receive the check by the law.
***Third**, mail the letter "return receipt" to ensure that the letter has arrived to its point of destination and the recipient has to sign that he or she has received the letter. In addition, mailing an item "return receipt" allows you to obtain an official record of the date, in which you requested the interest check.
***Last,** if you are moving make sure you leave your landlord a forwarding address, so that he can send you your deposit and interest check.

How Can I Request An Interest Check From My Security Deposit Before The Situation Escalates To An Eviction?

Under the current law, renters are not entitled to a security deposit refund, until the lease agreement has expired and the tenant has officially moved out of the rental unit. However, under the Landlord and Tenant Act, renters are entitled to request a check from the landlord, in which interest has accrued on the security deposit after a period of one year.
Therefore, if you want to avoid paying your rent late, you may want to ask your landlord or rental office for the interest that has accrued on your security deposit in order to pay your rent on time. However, keep in mind

that you do not have to tell your landlord why you want the check. Landlords/rental offices are required by law to return your interests on your deposit after you have requested it, and have done so in the time frame set forth by law, which is a period after one year.

An Important Note

To learn about the landlord and tenant laws in your state, please visit http://www.rentlaw.com/statelist.htm or http://www.rentlaw.com/securitydeposit.htm.

What Can I Do If My Landlord Refuses To Return My Security Deposit?

If your landlord refuses to return your security deposit, you can sue him in Small Claims Court. By law, your landlord must return your security deposit and/or send you an itemized list of deductions for damages done to the property within the time frame set forth by law. Second, you can seek advice by calling your local landlord and tenant court in the state, in which you reside, or you can search landlord and tenant laws by state at http://www.rentlaw.com.

The Federal Unemployment Tax Act (or **FUTA**, 26 U.S.C. ch.23[dead link])

"It is an United States federal law that imposes a federal employer tax used to fund state workforce agencies. Employers report this tax by filing an annual Form 940 with the Internal Revenue Service. In many cases, the employer is required to pay the tax in installments during the tax year," as noted by The Internal Revenue Service.

What Is Unemployment Insurance?

Unemployment insurance is compensation or financial assistance, which is paid through a federal-state unemployment program by an employer.

How Does Unemployment Work?

It is a federal mandate that all states provide unemployment benefits for those who have lost their jobs due to no fault of their own. Thereby, each state, of course following federal guidelines, is left to "determine the benefit amount and the length of time benefits are available," as noted by the Employment Security Department.

In most states, "The first four out of the last five completed calendar quarters prior to filing a claim are used to determine the weekly benefit amount and length of time a person is eligible to receive unemployment benefits," according to The Employment Security Department, To learn more about unemployment insurance, please visit http://www.esd.wa.gov.

How Can I Qualify For Unemployment Insurance?
*You must be physically and mentally able to work.

*You must be totally unemployed or slow worked, which meets the eligibility requirements to draw unemployment insurance.

*You must meet specific monetary requirements in terms of weekly earnings.

*You must have been separated from your place of employment for reasons not within your control and you must be registered with the Department of Employment Services and be available for work.

What Is Social Security?
The Social Security Act was signed into law by President Franklin D. Roosevelt in 1935, as it was introduced to Americans as The New Deal. In short, Social Security is a social insurance program, which provides income to persons of old-age who have retired from the work force. Also, the Act extends benefits to survivors, and persons who are disabled.

How Does Social Security Work?
The Social Security Administration is headquartered in Woodlawn, Maryland. Social Security is funded through federal payroll taxes, which both employer and employees pay through what is called, The Federal Insurance Contribution Act.

*Benefits are based on the number of credits a worker earns throughout his or her employment history.

*A person's date of birth determines the number of credits that must be earned prior to retiring.

*Any person born after 1929 must earn 40 credits in order to qualify for Social Security benefits.

What Are The Eligibility Requirements For Social Security?
*You must be 62 years of age, or older.

*You must earn ten 10 years work credits to be eligible for benefits.

*Benefits are based on the amount of money a person has earned during the course of their work history. To learn more about Social Security benefits, please visit Social Security Administration at http://www.socialsecurity.gov , or apply for Social Security benefits online at http://www.ssa.gov/onlineservices.

How Can I Work And Draw Social Security At The Same Time?
Yes, you can work and draw Social Security benefits at the same time. However, there is a limit of how much you can earn each year, without losing your Social "While you are working, your earnings will reduce your benefit amount only until you reach full retirement age," as noted by the Social Security Administration. "After you reach full retirement age, Social Security recalculates your benefit amount to leave out the months when it reduced or withheld benefits due to your excess earnings."
For more information, please visit the Social Security Retirement Planner at http://www.ssa.gov/retire2/whileworking.htm.

How Can I Receive Both Unemployment And Social Security When I Retire?
According to The Employment Security Department, you may be eligible to receive unemployment and Social Security benefits at the same time, but only for a specified period of time.

How Does Unemployment And Social Security Work?
"Unemployment insurance benefits are not counted under the Social Security annual earnings test and therefore do not affect your receipt of Social Security benefits. However, the unemployment benefit amount of an individual may be reduced by the receipt of a pension or other retirement income, including Social Security and Railroad Retirement benefits," as noted by the Social Security Administration, To learn more, please visit Social Security Administration at
 http://ssa-custhelp.ssa.gov/app/answers/detail/a_id/1705/~/receiving-social-security-and-unemployment-at-the-same-time, or visit http://workforcesecurity.doleta.gov/map.asp.

Can Non-Citizens Receive Social Security Benefits?

Yes, however, strict guidelines apply.

How Can Non-Citizens Qualify For Social Security Benefits?

Non-citizens must meet the same requirements as an U.S. citizen. However, as of January 1, 2004, a non-citizen or alien must also meet additional requirements in order to receive Social Security benefits. Requirements are as follows:

First, you must have been assigned a Social Security number on or after January 1, 2004. **Second,** you must prove that you was admitted to the U.S. as a nonimmigrant for business (B-1) or as an alien crewman (D-1 or D-2) **Third,** after both requirements have been met, it is further required that alien workers prove "lawful presence" of the beneficiary. Meaning, the alien must prove whether he or she was **(1) a U.S. Citizen, (2) a U.S. National; or (3) an alien lawfully present in the United States.**

An Important Note

Generally, those who qualify for SSI and SSD are not eligible to receive unemployment benefits. However, if you have additional questions, you can contact the Unemployment and Social Security Administration in your state.

Sources

Employment Security Department at   http://www.esd.wa.gov
U.S. Department of Labor: State Unemployment Insurance Benefits
U.S. Department of Labor at http://workforcesecurity.doleta.gov/unemploy.
National Employment Law Project: Unemployment Insurance and Social Security Retirement Offsets.

What Is Private Mortgage Insurance?

Private Mortgage Insurance protects the lender against losses if the buyer defaults on his or her loan. According to the Federal Trade Commission, cancelling your PMI Insurance can possibly save you hundreds of dollars each year.

Who Is Required To Pay Private Mortgage Insurance?

Homeowners that pay less than 20 percent down on a home mortgage are usually required to pay PMI Insurance, according to the Federal Trade Commission. In short, PMI coverage is what lenders require buyers to pay if the purchase of the home is more than 80 percent of the home's value.

How Can I Receive A Check From My Private Mortgage Insurance?

The Homeowner's Protection Act includes provisions for borrower-requested cancellation and automatic termination of Private Mortgage Insurance, as noted by the Federal Trade Commission. **First,** you have the right to cancel your private mortgage insurance when you pay your mortgage payments down to a point that equals 80 percent of the original purchase price or the appraised value of your home. **Second,** "The Homeowner's Protection Act of 1998 requires lenders to provide certain disclosures concerning PMI for loans secured by the consumer's primary residence obtained on or after July 29, 1999." **Third,** The Homeowner's Protection Act states "home mortgages signed on or after July 29, 1999, your PMI must - with certain exceptions - be terminated automatically when you reach 22 percent equity in your home based on the original property value, if your mortgage payments are current.," as noted by the Federal Trade Commission. To learn more, please visit FTC at http://www.ftc.gov/bcp/edu/pubs/consumer/alerts/alt072.shtm.

An Important Note

Government-insured FHA or VA loans or loans with lender-paid PMI are not protected under the Homeowners Protection Act, as stated by the Federal Trade Commission. For more information about rules and eligibility factors concerning Private Mortgage Insurance, please visit the http://www.frbsf.org/publications/consumer/pmi.html#cancel.

Sources

Federal Trade Commission
http://www.ftc.gov/bcp/edu/pubs/consumer/alerts/alt072.shtm
The National Reserve Bank of San Francisco at
http://www.frbsf.org/publications/consumer/pmi.html#cancel.

How Can I Request A Check or Tax Break For Stolen Property Due To A Natural Disaster?

The Internal Revenue Service (IRS) defines a natural disaster as, "A casualty loss can result from the damage, destruction or loss of your property from any sudden, unexpected, or unusual event such as a flood, hurricane, tornado, fire, earthquake or even volcanic eruption, and **theft** as, the taking and removing of money or property with the intent to deprive the owner of it. The taking must be illegal under the law of the state where it occurred and it must have been done with criminal intent."

An Important Note

The Disaster Tax Relief is covered by the IRS under Topic 515-Casualty, Disaster, and Theft Losses section.

Under The National Disaster Relief Act of 2008

The IRS explained the new changes as being "effective for losses attributable to disasters federally declared in taxable years beginning after December 31, 2007, and before January 1, 2010, which provides the following:

*It Allows all taxpayers, not just those who itemize, to claim the net disaster loss deduction regardless of the taxpayer's adjusted gross income.

*Removes the 10 percent of adjusted gross income limitation for net disaster losses.

*Provides a 5-year net operating loss (NOL) carry back for qualified disaster losses.

*Changes the amount by which all individual taxpayers must reduce their personal casualty or theft losses for each casualty or theft event from $100 to $500. This applies to deductions claimed in 2009. The reduction amount returns to $100 for taxable years beginning after December 31, 2009."

How Can I Receive A Check For Theft Resulting From National Disaster?

"In the case of <u>Gerstell (Petitioner) v. Commissioner of Internal Revenue (Respondent) 46 T.C. 161</u> (Docket No. 4299-64, filed May 4,1966)

(Exhibit "2"), the Tax Court States (at Page 7): Section 165 of the Internal Revenue Code of 1954 provides for the deduction of losses arising from theft. Therefore, if you have suffered losses from a national disaster, you may qualify for a tax break and also, be compensated for your losses." Simply, file a claim with the IRS using Form 4684 and Form 1040 Schedule A at http://www.irs.gov/pub/irs-pdf/f4684.pdf.

Who Is Eligible To File A Natural Disaster Claim?
Anyone who has suffered a lost due to vandalism, tornadoes, disaster-related demolition, earthquakes, floods, fires, hurricanes, shipwrecks, storms, terrorists attacks, and volcano eruptions, you may be eligible to receive a tax break and/or compensation for your losses of items that are not covered or claimed already by your personal insurance coverage.

What Types of Thefts And Losses Are Covered?
Larceny, extortion, burglary, blackmail, embezzlement or kidnapping for ransom. For more information about natural disaster claims, including tax law changes, please visit the Internal Revenue Service at http://www.irs.gov/taxtopics/tc515.html or visit Federal Emergency Management Agency (FEMA) at http://www.fema.gov.

Sources
The Internal Revenue Service at IRS.gov or at http://www.irs.gov/taxtopics/tc515.html. Also, see Publication 547, Casualties, Disasters, and Thefts, as provided by the IRS. Second to file a Publication 547 Form at http://www.irs.gov/pub/irs-pdf/p547.pdf. Federal Emergency Management Agency

---

How Can I Receive A Check From My Utility Company?
(Water, gas, and electric companies)
In New York, under the Home Energy Fair Practices Act, utility companies are required to pay interest on deposits. Also, utility companies are required to refund your deposit, plus the interest after one (1) year, if you have not been behind in rent payments. Nevertheless, utility companies can use your deposit to pay past due amounts, thereby, leaving you the remaining balance. Please check with your state's Public Utility Commission to see whether there is an existing law that requires utility companies to return your deposit with accrued interest. In short, utility companies are governed under The Public Utility Holding Company Act of 1935.

An Important Note

Utility companies are regulated by The Public Service Commission, which regulates the rates and services of a public utility. To learn more about the laws in your state, please visit Deposit Interest and Refund (Residential Consumer Rights about Deposits at http://www.constructionweblinks.com/Industry_Topics/Engineering_Environment/Infrastructure/utility_commissions/utility_commissions.html.

Sources

Pulp.TC Public Utility Law Project
http://archive.pulp.tc/html/history_of_hefpa.html
The Federal Trade Commission at
http://www.ftc.gov/bcp/edu/pubs/consumer/credit/cre22.shtm
Wikipedia The Free Encyclopedia

"Give Me Liberty Or Give Me Death"
Patrick Henry, March 23, 1775.

Photo: Public Domain- Patrick Henry 1736-99, political leader in the
American Revolution

Photo:: Public Domain - **Head of Statue of Liberty on display in park in Paris 1878 from Library of Congress** Photo
Originally by: Albert Fernique (born c. 1841, died 1898).

Photo: Public Domain -A photo of Uncle Sam with an empty treasury
(Uncle Sam is broke) Photo originally by James Montgomery Flagg in 1920.

Uncle Sam Wants Your Money

Are you going to let him take it?
He will, if you don't claim it first!

Chapter Seven
WHAT IS GOOD For The GOOSE
IS GOOD For The GANDER

(An American Proverb)

This chapter covers the following topics:

Monies Due You That Go Unclaimed

How To Purchase Government Assets At Wholesale Prices

*What Is Unclaimed Property?

*How Does Property Become Lost?

*What Happens To Property That Goes Unclaimed?

* How Much Does It Cost To Search The Unclaimed Property Website?

*How Does The State's Unclaimed Property Unit Locate Me?

*Search The National Registry of Unclaimed Retirement Benefits

*Search The Government's Unclaimed Property website

What Is Unclaimed Property?
*Travelers checks
*HUD/FHA Refunds
*Utility Deposits
*Royalty Payments
*Insurance Payments
*Land, Houses, Cars, and Money
*Money Orders, Federal Refund Checks
*Payroll Checks, and etc.

How Property Becomes Lost?
*Property can become lost by not leaving a forwarding address on record. Also, property can become lost through abandonment, such as the abandonment of packages, land, money, checking and savings, or through a forgotten safety deposit box.
*Property can become lost due to a name change, or through an insurance policy, in which you are the beneficiary, and no one knows how to contact you.

What Happens To Property That Goes Unclaimed?
The state's unclaimed property unit has millions of dollars in its registry that could belong to you. Yet, it goes unclaimed; because you are not aware it belongs to you. Therefore, there are unclaimed property laws that states must follow, which declare property is abandoned when inactivity appears three to five years. Afterwards, the unclaimed property is turned over to the state's unclaimed property unit.
If you desire to search the unclaimed registry, please visit http://www.unclaimed.org, or visit the U.S. Department of Treasury.

How Much Does It Cost To Search The Unclaimed Property Website?
It is absolutely free!

How Can The Unclaimed Property Unit Locate Me?
Generally, states locate property owners by placing an ad in the local newspaper, or by tracing the owner's last place of residency.

PURCHASE GOVERNMENT ASSETS AT WHOLESALE PRICES
A LIST OF GOVERNMENT RESOURCES

Government Sales and Auctions
http://www.usa.gov/shopping/shopping.shtml.

The Pension Benefit Guaranty Corporation
http://www.pbgc.gov.

Federal Deposit Insurance Corporation (FDIC)
Asset Sales (furniture, fixtures, and equipment)
http://www2.fdic.gov/funds/index.asp; or
http://www.fdic.gov/buying/otherasset/index.html.

U.S. Federal Investments
http://www.treasurydirect.gov/indiv/tools/tools_treasuryhunt.htm.

Missing U.S. Federal Savings Bonds and Other U.S. Securities
http://www.rbcbondsearch.com/bondsearch123.asp?categoryID=10&gclid
=COjew-bbpqUCFQY65Qod1yg94w; or at
http://www.rbcbondsearch.com/bonddesk/bonddeskframeset.htm..

U.S. Department of Housing and Urban Development Refund
http://www.hud.gov/offices/hsg/comp/refunds/index.cfm

Veterans Administration Benefits
http://www.va.gov

U.S. Railroad Retirement Board
http://www.rrb.gov.

Bid On Government Real Estate and Personal Property Sales
Federal Deposit Insurance Company
Purchase Commercial or Industrial Property at http://orelistings.cbre.com,
or at http://www.fdiclistings.com.

Internal Revenue Seized Property
http://usgovinfo.about.com/gi/dynamic/offsite.htm?site=http://www.treas.
gov/auctions/irs/index.html.

Bid On Government Property Daily
www.Aution.com.

Purchase One-Dollar Homes From HUD
Through The Good Neighbor Next Door Program
http://hudhomestore.com/HUDHome/GNND.aspx.

Nonprofits Purchase Homes Up To 30 Percent Discount
http://hudhomestore.com/HUDHome/NonprofitGovtAgency.aspx.

U.S. Custom Service
Purchase Seized Real Estate Sold By Public Auction.

Government Supplies and Other Equipment For Sale
http://www.usa.gov/shopping/supplies/supplies.shtml.

Government Homes and Auction Site
http://www.treasury.gov/auctions/treasury/rp/realprop.shtml.

U.S. Marshalls Seized and Forfeit Vehicles
http://www.cwsmarketing.com/USMScars.cfm.

U.S. Customs Abandoned or Unclaimed Merchandise For Sale
http://www.cwsmarketing.com/longbeach_onsite.cfm; or visit
http://www.usmarshals.gov/assets/sales.htm.

FCC License Auction
http://wireless.fcc.gov/auctions/default.htm?job=auctions_home.

Defense Logistics Agency
Military Supplies and Equipment
http://www.drms.dla.mil/sales.

United States Department of the Treasury
http://www.treas.gov/auctions.

Search Unclaimed Money Site By State
http://www.unclaimed.org.

Search The National Registry of Unclaimed Retirement Benefits
https://www.unclaimedretirementbenefits.com/NRSearchSSN.aspx.

Sources

A list of unclaimed property sites you can visit and search
at http://www.usa.gov/Citizen/Topics/Money_Owed.shtml.
and USA.gov, or the Federal Registry of Unclaimed Retirement Benefits
at https://www.unclaimedretirementbenefits.com.

Chapter Eight

A Dish Fit For The Gods
(By William Shakespeare)

This chapter covers the following topic:

Fifty Ways To Earn Quick Cash

*Consider starting a consulting business.

*Consider starting an online service (market your specialty)

*Consider becoming a part-time book vendor .

*Consider purchasing a vending machine or bubble gum machine, and then placing it in the Mall or department store to earn quick cash.

*Consider selling life insurance or investment portfolios.

*Consider working in pest control (exterminating rodents for commercial and residential clients).

*Consider starting a home repair business.

*Consider starting a shoe repair business.

*Consider starting a window cleaning business (contract with commercial and residential clients).

*Consider starting a landscaping business or lawn mowing service.

*Consider starting an accessory shop for men or women .

*Consider working as a painter painting houses.

*Consider selling flower arrangements or flower delivery.

*Consider producing and selling music beats to other artist.

*Consider working as a freelance photographer.

*Consider working as a freelance writer.

*Consider hosting a talent show (sale tickets for money).

*Consider managing plays (promote and sale theatre tickets for money).

*Consider hosting a poetry contest (charge for entry).

*Consider working as a tailor; make clothes, sew, or do alterations.

*Consider working as a Mary Kay or AVON consultant.

*Consider tutoring others using the Internet.

*Consider working as a sports referee.

*Consider working as a babysitter.

*Consider working as a part-time mechanic.

*Consider house sitting.

*Consider working as a movie extra.

*Consider working as a waiter or waitress.

*Consider driving a taxi cab part-time.

*Consider participating in market research surveys for cash.

*Consider having a yard sale.
*Consider having an estate sale.
*Consider selling iron scraps to the salvage yard.
*Consider pizza delivery.
*Consider newspaper delivery.
*Consider selling old car parts to the salvage yard.
*Consider hauling trash to the city dump.
*Consider working at a car wash or changing oil part-time.
*Consider working as a street performer on weekends for extra cash.
*Consider working as a food vendor.
*Consider selling bake goods on holidays or for special occasions.
*Consider selling dinners for extra cash.
*Consider hosting a fundraiser event and raffle off tickets for money.
*Consider cashing in your stocks and bonds.
*Consider borrowing against your 401(K) Plan.
*Consider cashing in your IRA or Annuity.
  *Consider cashing in your Whole Life Insurance policy.
*Consider applying for a cash advance.
*Consider visiting a Pond Shop for quick cash.
*Consider returning bottles or soda cans at the supermarket for cash.

Chapter Nine
MUM's The Word
(Shakespeare in Henry VI, Part II, 1592)

This chapter covers the following topics:
Quick Cash From Your Home, Car, And College

How Can I Earn Money From My Home?
*Consider a reversed mortgage.
*Consider cashing in your Real Estate Investment Trust.
*Consider starting a home day care business.
*Consider starting a home-based tax business.
*Consider starting a home-based catering service.
*Consider renting out a room in your home.
*Consider renting out your basement as an apartment.
*Consider applying for a home equity loan.
*Consider creating a home-based business.
 (foster care or home for the aging).
*Consider renting out rooms in your home as office space.
*Consider having an estate sale or yard sale.
*Consider cleaning fish for others for a fee.
*Consider renting out your kitchen to food vendors for food preparation or offer cooking classes teaching others how to cook.
*Consider making clothes at prom time, graduation, and weddings.

How Can I Earn Money From My Car?
*Consider starting a home-based auto repair shop.
*Consider flower delivery.
*Consider selling parts off your old car to the salvage yard.
*Consider driving a taxi part-time.
*Consider pizza delivery.
*Consider having a car wash.
*Consider changing oil for a fee.

*Consider installing car stereo systems for a fee.
*Consider providing detailing services for a fee.
*Consider hauling junk for others for a fee.
*Consider moving others for a fee.
*Consider detailing cars for a fee.
*Consider selling your car for quick cash.
*Consider providing driver lessons to others (tutor others).

How Can I Earn Money While I Am In College?
*Consider selling textbooks back to the college bookstore or sell your books on e-bay or online.
*Consider tutoring music, math, science, and computer technology.
*Consider working as an Intern.
*Consider working as a Fellow.
*Consider joining the Junior ROTC Program.
*Consider joining the Army Reserves.
*Consider working as a babysitter.
*Consider working as a security guard for your college.
*Consider working as a computer technician for your college.
*Consider working a campaign for a city, state, or national election.
*Consider working for a temporary agency.
*Consider participating in your school's work study program.
*Consider working as a teacher's assistant.
*Consider applying for scholarships, grants, and student loans.
*Consider applying for food stamps for those students who claim themselves and work at least 20 hours a week.

Section Two
MUM's The Word

An Online Employment Directory For College Students
Internships, Fellowships, and Employment Opportunities

StudentJOBs

Search the federal registry for internships, fellowships, and employment opportunities at http://www.students.gov/STUGOVWebApp/Public

USA Jobs Working For America

Search national registry for student jobs
http://www.usajobs.gov/studentjobs

USA Jobs Working For America

Search for federal employment according to college major
http://www.usajobs.gov/EI/jobsbycollegemajor.asp#icc

U.S. Office Of Personnel Management
Federal Hiring Flexibilities Resource Center For Student Employment

Apply for fellowships and scholarships
http://www.opm.gov/Strategic_Management_of_Human_Capital/fhfrc/FLX04020.asp

Federal Career Internship Program

Search employment registry
Apply for career intern positions
http://www.opm.gov/careerintern

Student Temporary Employment Program (STEP)

Offers temporary employment opportunities for students
Employment for degree-seeking students
http://www.usajobs.gov/EI/students.asp#icc

Student Career Employment Program (SCEP)

Offers work experience that is directly related to your field of study.
Employment for degree-seeking students
http://www.usajobs.gov/EI/students.asp#icc.

Presidential Management Fellows Program
https://www.pmf.opm.gov

Senate Placement Office
Employment opportunities
http://www.senate.gov/visiting/common/generic/placement_office.htm

Senate Employment Resume Bank And Employment Bulletin
Employment opportunities
http://www.senate.gov/pagelayout/visiting/h_multi_sections_and_teasers/employment.htm., or visit
http://www.senate.gov/employment/po/positions.htm.

U.S. House Of Representatives
Employment opportunities
http://www.house.gov/cao-hr

U.S. Supreme Court Fellows Program
http://www.supremecourt.gov/fellows

White House (The)
Internship opportunities
http://www.whitehouse.gov/about/internships/apply

White House (The)
Fellowships
http://clinton2.nara.gov/WH_Fellows

Workforce Recruitment Program (WRP)
It is a job placement program for college students with disabilities provided by the U.S. Department of Labor's Office of Disability Employment Policy at http://www.dol.gov/odep/programs/workforc.htm

Indeed.com
Search for jobs nationally
Register and have job notices sent to your email address.
http://www.indeed.com

Careerbuilder.com
Register with Career builder and have job notices sent to your email address. Register at

http://www.careerbuilder.com/Jobs/Company/C8B86T65NXQGDZTW2F
V/NATIONAL-COLLEGE-Jobs

College Recruiter
Search national job registry
http://collegerecruiter.com

Common Good Careers
Search nonprofit jobs
http://www.cgcareers.org

Cub Reporters
Search national registry for paid internships, fellowships, journalism , and
broadcast jobs.
http://cubreporters.org

Federal Jobs By College Major
Majorhttp://www.usajobs.gov/EI/jobsbycollegemajor.asp#icc

Political Jobs On And Off Capitol Hill
http://www.hillzoo.com

Sargeant At Arms Job Listings
http://www.senate.gov/employment/saa/positions.htm

U.S. Department Of State Student Career Jobs And Internships
http://www.careers.state.gov/students/programs.html

Jobs For Veterans Act
http://www.doleta.gov/programs/VETs

Employment Training And Opportunities For Native Americans
U.S. Department Of Labor
http://www.doleta.gov/DINAP

U.S. Department Of Justice
Student Programs and Internships
http://www.justice.gov/careers/student_programs.html

Chapter Ten
Another Day, Another Dollar
(An 1897 Quote linked to J. Conrad *Nigger of 'Narcissus'* (1955)
v. 114, but dates as far back as 1867)

This chapter covers the following topic:
 Money via Internet
*Create An Online Store

*Create A Business Blog

*Create An eBay Business

* Create An e-Commerce Business

*Create An Online Book Publishing Company

*Create A Franchise (purchase vending machines, bubble gum machines place them in the Mall or in stores).

*Create An Online eBook Store

*Create An Online Graphics Business

*Create An Online Consulting Business

*Design And Sell Website Templates Online

*Design And Sell Business Cards Online.

*Design And Sell Greeting Cards Online.

*Create A Photo Gallery And Sell Your Photos Online

*Create A Music Site And Sell Beats Online

*Create An Online Store And Sell merchandise

Chapter Eleven
A Good Name Is Better Than Silver Or Gold
(Proverbs 22:1 KJV)

This chapter covers the following topic:
How To Pay Off Bad Debt And Charge Smart
This chapter introduces smart ways to use your pre-paid credit and debit cards. Also, this chapter will help you become familiar with the credit laws that empower you.

What Is The Fair Credit Reporting Act?
The Fair Credit Reporting Act was signed into law in 1970. The Act regulates the collection, dissemination, and use of consumer information that is released about you to others.

What Is The Equal Credit Opportunity Act?
The Equal Credit Opportunity Act was signed into law in 1974. The Act prohibits discrimination against being denied credit based on a person's sex, race, religion, marital status, national origin, age, or recipient of public welfare.

What Is The Fair Debit Collection Practices Act?
The Fair Debit Collection Practices Act was signed into law 1978. The Act forbids debt collectors from using abusive, deceptive or unfair practices to collect a debt. Also, the Act provides consumers a legal avenue to dispute a debt, or obtain information about a debt.
Second, the Act regulates the conduct of bill collectors, and any institution that is in pursuit of collecting a debt. In short, even when you owe a legitimate debt, bill collectors must remain in compliance with the law. If they violate it, you can file a complaint with your state's attorney general office and the Federal Trade Commission. For more information, please visit http://ftc.gov/bcp/edu/pubs/consumer/credit/cre18.shtm.

What Debts Are Covered Under The Fair Debt Collection Act?
Generally, personal, family, household, medical and credit card debts are covered under the Act.

What Is The American Recovery and Reinvestment Act?

The American Recovery and Reinvestment Act is an economic stimulus package that was signed into law on February 13, 2009. The Act is a copulation of laws created to help give low to moderate income families tax breaks in order to offset the recession. For example, America's low-income families and small businesses could benefit in the following areas.

*An Expanded Earned Income Tax Credit
*An Expanded Child Tax Credit
*An Expanded College Credit
*Earned Income Credit
*Home Buyers And Home Energy Credit
*The American Opportunity Tax Credit and for businesses,
*The Work Opportunity Pay Tax Credit and the
*Making Work Pay Tax Credit, including a host of other credits.
To learn more, please visit www.federalhousingtaxcredit.com, or visit http://www.irs.gov/newsroom/article/0,,id=204335,00.html.

Sources

Federal Trade Commission
http://www.ftc.gov/os/statutes/031224fcra.pdf
http://www.ftc.gov/credit
The Internal Revenue Service at www.irs.gov; or
www.irs.gov/pub/irs-pdf/p919.pdf (Publication 919)
The IRS Center for Economic Progress
The American And Recovery Reinvestment Act of 2009
 at http://www.irs.gov/newsroom/article/0,,id=204335,00.html.
Tax Policy Center, and report by Senate Finance and House Ways and
 Means Committees Compiled April 2009.

What Is The Credit Repair Organization Act?

The Credit Repair Organization Act was signed into law in 1996. The Act was created to deter fraud throughout the Credit Repair Industry. To learn more, please visit the Federal Trade Commission at http://www.ftc.gov/ro/chro/credit.shtm , or visit http://www.ftc.gov/os/statutes/croa/croa.shtm.

What Are Alternative Ways To Pay Off Bad Debt?
(Irene's survival tips)

Purchase a pre-paid Visa or pre-paid debit card, and add the exact amount of money that you need to pay off the debt. By doing this, bill collectors cannot gain access to your personal account numbers. However, if you have a Savings account, bill collectors have been known to take legal action to take money from your savings to cover the unpaid debt. Also, if you are working, bill collectors have been known to take legal action to garnish wages. In short, this is a method that you can use to prevent bill collectors from gaining illegal access to your personal checking and savings accounts. Also, this method prevents collectors from having continuous access to your account and personal financial information.

What Are Other Benefits In Paying Off Debt
With A Pre-Paid Credit or Debit Card?
*It prevents bill collectors from withdrawing more money than you authorized.
*It provides an official record of the date, the day, and the month, in which the debt was paid.

How Can I Avoid Late Fees?
You can avoid late fees by purchasing a pre-paid Visa or pre-paid debit card to pay your bills.
The day you use your pre-paid debit or pre-paid debit card to pay your bills, actually becomes the official date of record, in which the debt was paid. Thereby, paying your bills with a pre-paid debit or credit card adjudicates an electronic payment, which is instantly recorded, opposed to the traditional way of sending payments through the mail that could pose a delay and cause your payment to be late. As a result, you are charged a late fee due to no fault of your own.

Second, by using a pre-paid Visa or pre-paid debit card, bill collectors cannot say that your payment was late, they cannot hold your payment back in order to make your payment appear late, and they cannot say that your payment got lost in the mail, because you will have documented proof of the payment on your billing statement

Third, by using a pre-paid credit card or pre-paid debit card to pay your bills, prevent creditors, again from gaining access to your personal Checking and Savings account.

Last, if you choose not to use a pre-paid debit or prepaid credit card to pay your bills, such as your utility, telephone, or credit card bills, you always have the option of paying your bill five to ten days in advanced , as a way to avoid late charges, but why be inconvenienced when you can just call your payment in and avoid all the Hassel.

How Can I Pay On The Principal And Less On Interests?
Simply pay your creditors by writing a personal check; or by issuing a cashier's check and endorse it as if it was a contract, instead of a mere transaction. Meaning, in the check's memo section write, "This check in the amount of ($100.00) for example, is payment on account # (""""), in which payment is to be credited towards the principal only."

Second, turn the check over and endorse the back of it and write "To (company's name) upon accepting, depositing, or cashing this check, you agree that this payment for the amount of "$100" is to be credited towards the principal only. Once this is done, the check now becomes a legal and binding document, and the creditor or bill collector must honor it, if the check was cashed, deposited the check, or cash the check.

How Can I Avoid Additional Fees When I Wire Money?
You can avoid late fees by not using wire services. Instead, set up a PayPal account, so others can deposit money directly into your account. Second, you can avoid bank fees, wire fees, or service fees when receiving money, as no fees are required to make a PayPal transaction. Honestly, I do not believe in paying money to get money. So, think smart! Send and receive money without going broke.

How Can I Create A PayPal Account?
Setting up a Pay Pal account is free via Internet at https://www.paypal.com.

How Can I Save Money When I Make A Cash Advance Transaction?
When making a cash advance transaction, pay only one fee. When you make a cash advance transaction have your bank deposit/transfer the money into your savings account, instead of giving you the money directly. Afterwards, withdraw the money from your savings account, which is a free transaction. This way you are paying only one fee for making the transaction, which is usually charged by the credit card issuer. Try it! See if this works for you (**This concludes Irene's tax tips**).

An Important Note
The Act prohibits the following collection practices, which are considered

abusive and deceptive: communication with third parties, who reveal or discuss your debts with others, except the consumer's spouse or attorney. *Hours of phone contact, usually bill collectors are not allowed to call you before 8a.m. or after 9p.m., which includes calling you excessively. . *Failure to cease communication upon your request, contacting your place of employment and talking to others about your debt, threatening arrest or legal action that is not legal, use of abusive or profane language, reporting false information on your credit report, and etc. To learn more, please visit FTC at http://www.ftc.gov/bcp/edu/pubs/consumer/credit/cre27.pdf.

Who Should I Contact About My Credit History?
You should contact the three major credit bureaus, which are
*Equifax: 1-800-525-628,
*Experian: 1-888-397-3742, and
*TransUnion at 1-800-680-7289

Sources
Tax Policy Center, and report by Senate Finance and House Ways and Means Committees Compiled April 2009, and the The Federal Trade Commission at http://www.ftc.gov/bcp/edu/pubs/consumer/credit/cre18.shtm.
The Free Merriam-Webster Dictionary

Chapter Twelve
No Weapons Formed Against Me Shall Prosper
(Isaiah 54:17 KJV)

This chapter covers the following topic:

How To Guard Against Identity Theft?

According to the Federal Deposit Insurance Corporation (FDIC), "Identity theft continues to be one of the fastest growing crimes in the United States, and has ranked as one of the top consumer concerns for the past several years." The Federal Trade Commission advises the following to minimize identity theft:

*Be mindful of what you throw in the trash.

*Be cautious when using your personal identification over the Internet.

*Make sure you verify a source before sharing your information.

*Store sensitive information in a secure place.

* Make sure you request a credit freeze, if your identity has been compromised.

*Always safeguard your purse and wallet.

How Can I Freeze My Credit If My Identity Has Been Compromised?

The Federal Trade Commission explained there are several states that allow consumers to "freeze" their credit. Meaning, credit agencies can place restrictions on opening new lines of credit at the consumer's request, as well as prevent the authorization of new credit charges on your existing accounts. By doing this, FTC says "It's unlikely that an identity thief would be able to open a new account in your name."

For additional information, please visit the website below to check your state's "credit freeze" laws at

http://www.consumersunion.org/campaigns/learn_more/003484indiv.html.

How Can I Detect That My Identity Has Been Compromised?

FTC offers the following ways you can detect whether your identity has been compromised:

"*Accounts you didn't open and debts on your accounts that you can't explain.

*Fraudulent or inaccurate information on your credit reports, including accounts and personal information, like your social security number, address, name or initials, and employers.

*Failing to receive bills or other mail. Follow up with creditors if your bills don't arrive on time.

*A missing bill could mean that an identity thief has taken over your account and perhaps, changed your billing address to cover his or her tracks.

*Receiving credit cards in which you did not apply.

*Being denied credit or being offered less favorable credit terms, like a high interest rate, for no apparent reason.

*Getting calls or letters from debt collectors or businesses about merchandise or services you didn't buy."

How Can I Report Scams, Fraud, And Hoaxes?
*Search whether a website or website information is fake or genuine, please visit http://www.who.is/website-information
*Reporting scams fraud, and hoaxes to the FBI at http://www.consumerfraudreporting.org/FBI_LocalOffices.php.
*Learn who owns the site, owner's email address, telephone number, street address, date the site was created, how long site has been online, and etc. http://www.who.is, or visit http://www.consumerfraudreporting.org/identity.php.
*Protect yourself against identity theft by purchasing identity theft insurance at http://www.nextadvisor.com/identity_theft_protection_services/offer2.php?hl=2&kw=LPID2+gida+identity%20theft%20coverage, or visit FTC's website concerning identity theft insurance at http://www.fmaonline.org/uploadedFiles/Governmental_Affairs/files/FPIC_Red_Flags_rule_info.pdf.

How Can I Familiar Myself With Laws That Protect Me And Laws That Make Businesses And Institutions Accountable?
The Gramm-Leach-Bliley (GLB) Act, which was signed into law

November 12, 1999, requires companies to ensure the security and confidentiality of consumers' personal information by taking precautionary measures that would help safeguard against identity thieves, as noted by Federal Trade Commission. For more information, please visit the Federal Trade Commission at http://www.ftc.gov/bcp/edu/microsites/idtheft/business/safeguards.html.

Second, The Fair Credit Reporting Act
"Under the 2003 amendments to the **Fair Credit Reporting Act** (PDF, 192 KB) (FCRA) section 609(e), identity theft victims are entitled to get from businesses a copy of the application or other business transaction records relating to their identity theft free of charge," as noted by the Federal Trade Commission. For more information about identity theft tools, please visit http://www.ftc.gov/bcp/edu/microsites/idtheft/tools.html.

What Other Things Can I Do To Help Guard Against Identity Theft?
*You can make photo copies of your personal identification.
*Avoid using account information or your personal Identification online to suspicious websites.
*If you did not request a service or product do not buy it.
*If you did not apply for a job, do not respond to the drop-in adds online.
*Also, it helps to change the password on accounts regularly.
*Make sure to file a complaint about suspicious websites at http://www.bbb.org/us/article/ftc--information-compromise-and-the-risk-of-identity-theft-guidance-for-your-business-4561.

Sources
The Federal Deposit Insurance Corporation (FDIC)
To learn more about identity theft, please visit FDIC's website at http://www.fdic.gov/consumers/consumer/guard/.
Federal Trade Commission (FTC)
http://www.ftc.gov/bcp/edu/microsites/idtheft/ or contact the Better Business Bureau at http://www.bbb.org/.

Chapter Thirteen
Talk To The Hand Because The Face Ain't Listening
(Urban Slang)

This chapter covers the following topic:
How Can I Stop Bill Collectors And Telemarketers From Calling Me?
The Federal Trade Commission Guidelines and Laws
since February 2009.

The Federal Trade Commission
What Is Its Purpose?
The nation's Consumer Protection Agency, under The Fair Debt
Collection Practices Act (FDCPA) prohibits debt collectors from using
abusive, unfair, or deceptive practices in order to collect a debt.

What Is The Fair Debt Collection Practices Act?
It is a federal law that provides guidelines for collection agencies or bill
collectors that are seeking to collect a legitimate debt, while protecting the
rights of the debtor. Also, the Act prohibits debt collectors from using
unwarranted behavior, abusive language, unfair and/or deceptive practices
in order to collect a debt.

An Important Note
If you owe a debt, bill collectors have the legal right to call you, but they
do not have the right to harass you.

What Type Of Debts Are Covered Under The Act?
The Act covers personal, family, and household debts, including money
you owe on personal credit cards, auto loans, medical bills, or mortgage.
The FDCPA doesn't cover debts you incurred to run a business.

Can Bill Collectors Call Me Any At Time?
Under The Fair Debt Collection Practices Act, collection agencies cannot
make repeated telephone calls or call you at unreasonable times. Meaning,
the Act stipulates contacting a person before 8:00 a.m. or after 9:00 p.m. ,

unreasonable times, unless the consumer agrees to it. Also, bill collectors cannot contact you at work, unless you authorize them to do so.

How Can I Stop Bill Collectors From Calling Me?
You can stop bill collectors from calling you by telling them to stop calling you, and also by sending them a Cease and Desist letter.

What Is A Cease And Desist Letter?
"It is an order or request to halt an activity (cease) and not to take it up again later (desist); or else face legal action," as noted by Wikipedia The Online Encyclopedia.

How Does It Work?
Send a letter by certified mail and request a "return receipt," as proof that a written letter was sent to the bill collector. Once collectors receive the notice, they cannot legally continue to contact you, but if you owe the debt, collectors can take legal action to collect the debt. However, they are still prohibited from harassing you.

What Can I Do When I Do Not Owe The Debt?
You should send the bill collector a letter stating that you do not owe the debt, as well as enclose any verification proving you do not owe the debt. By doing this, the bill collector should honor it and thereby, stop calling you. However, if the bill collector continues to notify you about the debt, you should contact a major credit agency and have them reported.

Can Federal Benefits Be Garnished?
Many federal benefits are exempt from garnishment, such as in the following instances:

- Supplemental Security Income cannot be garnished, because the federal government funds it through general tax revenues. However, Social Security Disability Income (SSDI) can be garnished for child support since money is paid to recipients through the Social Security Trust Fund via employment taxes.

- Veteran Disability benefits can be garnished for child support and alimony payments. To learn more, please visit The U.S. Department of Health and Human Services under the Office of Child Support Enforcement at http://www.acf.hhs.gov/programs/cse/pol/IM/1998/im-9803.htm or visit The U.S. Department of Energy at https://www.directives.doe.gov/directives/current-directives/323.1-BOrder-ac1/view?searchterm=None to learn more about the garnishments of federal employees .

- Civil Service and federal retirement disability benefits are protected against garnishments. Also, this includes, Military Annuities and Survivors' benefits, Student Assistance, and Railroad Retirement benefits. According to the Defense Finance and Accounting Service in Cleveland, only the retiree's disposable retired pay is subject to garnishment. To learn more, please visit http://www.military.com/benefits/military-pay/retired-pay/pay-garnishment.

- Merchant Seamen Wages, Longshoremen's and Harbor Workers' Death and Disability Benefits are protected against garnishment.

- Also, Foreign Service Retirement and Disability benefits, Compensation for Injury, Death or Detention of Employees of U.S. Contractors outside the U.S., Federal Emergency Management Agency Federal Disaster Assistance are protected against garnishment. To learn more about restrictions on garnishments, please visit http://www.fair-debt-collection.com/garnishment-law.html or visit http://www.fair-debt-collection.com/garnishment-law.html#1.

An Important Note

Federal benefits can be garnished for delinquent taxes, alimony, child support, and student loans. However, to help guard against other types of garnishments, such as private and commercial garnishments, one should consider opening a separate bank account apart from the other monies that you receive. By placing your benefit check in a Savings & Loan savings account, usually prevents the first $500 from being garnished.

How Can I Report Bill Collectors Who Violate My Rights?

You can report violations to the State Attorney General's office at www.naag.org, or you can file a complaint with the Federal Trade Commission at http://www.ftc.gov/ftc/complaint.shtm . Although FTC does not represent individuals parse, it is known for taking legal action against bill collectors who harass consumers.

How Can I Stop Bill Collectors From Calling My Cell Phone?

Today, there are over 190 million Americans who own a cellular phone, which is more than the number of people who own a land-line phone. As a result, Forty-four states now have laws to protect cellular users from receiving harassing or threatening calls, according to Cellular Telecommunications International Association.

Steps To Stop Bill Collectors From Accessing Your Cell Phone:

Step 1. You can use the cell phone's "Call-Block" feature by selecting the "Selective Call-Block" prompt located on your cell phone).

Step 2. You can file a complaint with the Federal Communications Commission at http://www.ftc.gov/ftc/complaint.shtm.

Step 3. You can send bill collectors a letter, in which the Federal Trade Commission provides to notify bill collectors to stop calling you. Please view the sample letter provided on the next page for your convenience.

Sources

Cell Phone Privacy Rights at http://www.privacyrights.org/taxonomy/term/155.
National Do Not Call Registry at https://www.donotcall.gov.
Social Security Administration at http://www.ssa.gov.
Privacy Rights Clearinghouse: Empowering Consumers. Protecting Privacy
U.S. Department of Treasury/Comptroller of the Currency Administrator of National Banks at http://www.helpwithmybank.gov/faqs/banking_garnish.html.

FREE SAMPLE LETTER TO STOP DEBT COLLECTOR CALLS

(Provided by Federal Trade Commission and the Fair Debt Collection Practices Act)

Today's Date

Your Name
Your Address
Collector's Name
Collector's Address
Mr./Ms. Collector

I am writing in response to your constant harassing phone calls!
According to the Fair Debt Collection Practices Act, [15 USC 1692c] Section 805(c):
CEASING COMMUNICATION: You must, by law cease contacting me after being notified in writing that I no longer wish to communicate with you. **Therefore, I demand that you stop calling me!**

Also, in accordance with the federal FDCPA, now that you have received this official written notice "stop call" letter, I will only allow you to contact me if:

*propose to Terminate further collection efforts or
*propose a remedy within reason

Any further contact from your company or any third party collectors that you authorize to contact me will only violate the "FDCPA" law pertaining to section 805(b)2 of the FDCPA.

Please be advised, if you continue calling me I will take every legal action possible to stop your continued unwarranted calls.

Signature
Your Printed Name

An Important Note
Always send 'stop call' letters by official mail – Return Receipt Requested.

Source
The Federal Trade Commission at www.ftc.gov.
Fair Debt Collection Practices Act

Section Two

Talk To The Hand Because The Face Ain't Listening

How Can I Take Affirmative Action When Bill Collectors or Telemarketers Continue To Call Me?

Under the Do-Not-Call Improvement Act of 2007, "Telephone numbers placed on the National Do –Not-Call Registry will remain on the list, permanently," as noted by the Federal Trade Commission.

What Is The National Do Not Call Improvement Act?

The Act gives consumers the power they need to block unwanted calls from bill collectors, telemarketers, and etc. To learn more about the Act, please visit FTC at http://www.ftc.gov/opa/2008/04/dncfyi.shtm or visit http://www.ftc.gov/bcp/edu/pubs/consumer/alerts/alt107.shtm.

How Can I Register My Home and Cellular Number On The Do-Not-Call Registry?

*It is free to place a telephone number on the Do-Not-Call Registry.
*You can register your home or cellular number on the "Do- Not -Call Registry" at https://www.donotcall.gov/register/reg.aspx , or you can file a complaint with the Federal Trade Commission at www.fcc.gov/cgb/complaints.html.
*Also, you can register your home or cellular number by telephone at 1-888-382-1222. However, you must call from the telephone number that you desire to block incoming calls, as noted by the Federal Trade Commission.

An Important Note

After you have registered with "The National Do- Not-Call Registry," you should stop receive telemarketing calls after 31 days of registering your telephone number. However, if calls persist, you can always file a complaint with the Federal Trade Commission or with the registry at www.donotcall.gov.

How Can I File A Complaint Against Businesses In A Foreign Country?

You can file a cross-the-border consumer complaint at http://www.econsumer.gov/english or econsumer.gov.

How Can I Stop Harassing Text Messages?

*You can disable the text message feature on your cell phone.

*You can visit the Federal Communications Commission at http://www.fcc.gov/cgb/policy/DomainNameDownload.html to view the cellular domain name registry and to request a stop on unwanted commercial text messages to your cell phone.

*You can file a complaint with the Federal Communications Commission at www.fcc.gov/cgb/complaints.html, or email FCC at fccinfo@fcc.gov.

How Can I Block Unwanted Emails and Domains?

You can block unwanted emails and domains by using a service called, Boxbe.

What Is Boxbe?

Boxbe is a service that screens emails and minimizes email overloads by blocking unwanted domains and emails, in which you authorize.

How Does Boxbe Work?

*Currently, you can set up a Boxbe account free of charge.

*You can create an account online at http://www.boxbe.com.

*Once your account has been set up, all you need to do is set up your email guest list and you are well on your way in minimizing your email overload.

How Does Boxbe Block Unwanted Emails?

Emails that are delivered to your inbox are only sent to you upon your request. Thereby, mail only goes to your inbox if the following apply:

- "You have added the sender or the domain as a guest

- The sender makes a simple robot-proof request

- The message is under your customizable junk rating threshold

- The message is from a contact of a friend."

Further, Boxbe places new emails and domains into a temporary file or in your spam folder for approximately 30 days.

How Long Does Boxbe Hold Messages In The Temporary Storage Area?
*If you do not take action to approve new email or domain request, Boxbe will delete them. Messages are deleted 30 days after they are received.

New Email Guest Request (How Does It Work)?
People that you send messages to already are automatically added to your recipient guest list by Boxbe . Meaning, you will automatically receive emails from your pre-approved guest list, no questions asked.
* New guest alerts are automatically sent to your inbox for your approval or disapproval.
* Guests can be added in bulk, as well as individually.

What Are The Eligibility Requirements To Set Up A Boxbe Account?
*You must be 13 years old.
*You must have an existing email account.

What Emails Can Boxbe Support?
*Yahoo
*Mail
*Gmail
*Google Apps
*AOL Mail
*As for email accounts provided by cable providers, Boxbe can provide services to you, but you have to set up a public email account using Boxbe. In other words, your email address must be connected to a Boxbe address, which looks something like this, yourpersonalemailaddress@boxbe.com.

Sources

For more information about harassing calls and text messages, please visit The Federal Communications Commission prohibited text messages website at www.fcc.gov/policy/DomainNameDownload.html, or visit FCC 's Consumer Facts On Spam And Cell Phones www.fcc.gov/cgb/consumerfacts/canspam.html.
The Federal Trade Commission at http://www.ftc.gov/bcp/edu/pubs/consumer/alerts/alt107.shtm.
Boxbe at http://www.boxbe.com.

Photo: Public Domain President George Washington,
Originally by **Gilbert Stuart (1755–1828), Rembrandt Peale (1778–1860)**
painting (oil on canvas) of George Washington (1732–99).

The first president of the United States said, **"Bad seed is a robbery of the worst kind: for your pocketbook not only suffers by it, but your reparations are lost and a season passes away unimproved."** However, what I have come to admire most about George Washington was his unique ability in understanding seed time and harvest. George Washington said, **"Worry is the interest paid by those who borrow trouble,"** but **"Liberty, when it begins to take root, is a plant of rapid growth."**

Chapter Fourteen

YOU REAP WHAT YOU SOW
(Galatians 6:7-9 KJV)

This chapter covers the following topics:

Checking And Savings Accounts That Yield You Cash
*Bank Smart
*Benefits In Banking With FDIC
*Benefits In Investing In Money-Market Accounts

What Is The Federal Deposit Insurance Corporation (FDIC)?
*The FDIC Bank was created as part of the Glass-Steagall Act in 1933 to promote stability and public confidence in the nation's banking system.
*A FDIC Bank is a federal deposit insurance corporation.
*A FDIC Bank is charted by federal and state governments.
*A federally insured bank must display the official FDIC seal at each teller window, windows, and doors.

What Is The Purpose of FDIC Deposit Insurance?
*FDIC deposit insurance covers deposits dollar-for-dollar.
*FDIC insures deposits up to $250,000 if a loss, theft, or bank closing occurs. However, on January 1, 2014, limits will decrease to the standard insurable amount, which is $100,000 per depositor, except on Individual Retirement Accounts. IRA's will remain insurable at $200,000.
*FDIC insures a deposit up until the point a bank closes.

Who Does FDIC Insure?
*A FDIC Bank insures deposits, member banks, and thrifts up to $100,000.
*You do not have to be a U.S. citizen or resident of the United States to be insurable. However, FDIC only covers or insure depositors.

An Important Note
A FDIC Bank does not insure creditors or shareholders even though they might be depositors.

What Type of Accounts Are Covered By FDIC Bank?
*FDIC covers checking, savings, money market deposit accounts, and time deposits, such as (CD's), which is a certificate of deposit.

What Is Considered A Bank Failure?
A bank failure is the closing of a bank by a federal or state banking regulatory agency.

What Is FDIC'S Role When A Bank Fails?
* FDIC is the insurer of the bank's deposits.
*FDIC pays insurance up to the insurance limit of the deposit.
* FDIC assumes the task of selling and collecting bank assets, as well as settling bank debts.

How Will I know When My Bank Closes?
*FDIC notifies depositors as soon as their bank closes.
*FDIC contacts each depositor in writing.

How Can I Participate In FDIC's Asset Sales?
* You can visit FDIC's website at http://www.fdic.gov/buying.
*Gain insight about loans, real estate sales, and other asset or property sales at http://www2.fdic.gov/drrore, or visit
 http://www.fdiclistings.com/ or http://orelistings.cbre.com.

*You can visit FDIC's official website, at http://www.fdic.gov , or you can contact FDIC's Call Center at 1-877-275-3342.
*To contact FDIC's Affordable Housing Program, please visit http://www.fdic.gov/buying/owned/affordable/affordable/ahcontacts.html.

Sources
USA.gov
Federal Deposit Insurance Corporation
Freedom of Information Act (FOIA) Service Center
FDIC Office of Inspector General
FDIC Open Government Webpage

Chapter Fifteen

HOME SWEET HOME
(A 150 year-old song adapted by actor John Howard Payne's in 1823)

This chapter covers the following topics:

Ways To Purchase A Home Without Losing It To Foreclosure
*HUD's 203(k) Government Grants for Homes and Investment Property
*Land Contract Homes
*Hybrid Adjustable Rate Mortgage (ARMs)
*ARMS Mortgage
*Fixed Rate Mortgage
*Conventional Loan
*FHA Loan
*VA Loan
*Purchase Home by Auction
*Purchase Foreclosure Homes
*Mortgage- Backed Securities
*Mortgage -Backed Bonds

What Is A HUD 203(k) Rehab Plan?
*This is a plan that offers government grants for homes and investment properties.
*Money is granted to rehabilitate buildings and single-family homes.
*The Federal Housing Administration (FHA) offers
the HUD 203 (k) program to rehabilitate and repair single unit family homes, as a way to expand the opportunity of homeownership.
*Also, you can apply for a loan through HUD's Home, Hope and Community Development Block Grants.

How Can I Purchase A HUD 203 (K) Rehab Home?
You can purchase a rehab home through the HUD 203(K) Rehab Program.
*First, you must obtain financing to purchase the dwelling.
*Second, you may need to acquire additional financing to rehabilitate the construction of the home.
*Third, a permanent mortgage is required "when the work is completed to pay off the interim loans with a permanent mortgage, as noted by the Department of Housing and Urban Development.
To learn more about HUD's 203 (K) Program, please visit
http://www.hud.gov/offices/hsg/sfh/203k/203kabou.cfm.

An Important Note
What Is The Community Reinvestment Act?
The Community Reinvestment Act was enacted by Congress in 1977. The Act was "Intended to encourage depository institutions to meet the needs of borrowers in all segments of their communities, including low- to-moderate-income neighborhoods," as defined by Wikipedia, an online dictionary. Also, the Act was "Designed to reduce discriminatory credit practices against low-income neighborhoods, a practice known as redlining."

What Is A Land Contract?
A land contract is an agreement between the seller and the buyer, in which the seller holds the title on the home until the buyer pays the set agreed price in-full.

How Can I Purchase A Home On Land Contract?
To request a listing of land contract homes, or to purchase a home on land contract, please visit the links below:
www.TheLandContract.com
www.AllHud.net

What Is A Hybrid Adjustable Rate Mortgage?
A Hybrid Adjustable Rate Mortgage provides a fixed mortgage payment for a few years and afterwards, changes to an adjustable loan.

What Is An ARMS Mortgage?
Usually, an ARMS Mortgage has a fixed- interest rate at first and then, it becomes an adjustable rate mortgage, in which payments change over time.

What Is A Fixed Rate Mortgage?
A Fixed-Rate Mortgage is a mortgage that has a fixed interest rate for the entire term of the loan.

What Is A Conventional Loan?
Usually, a Conventional Loan, offers a fixed-interest rate, in which the interests rate remains the same throughout the term of the loan. Also, a conventional loan is not insured or guaranteed by the federal government.

What Is A FHA Loan?
A Federal Housing Administrative Mortgage (FHA) is a mortgage issued by a federal lender, which is insured by the Federal Housing

Administration.

What Is A VA Loan?
A VA loan is a mortgage loan established by the U.S. Department of Veteran Affairs for U.S. service members desiring to purchase a home. Usually, VA loans require no down payment.

How Can I Purchase A Home By Auction?
Homes are auctioned to the highest bidder by way of a public auction. Usually, purchasing a home by auction does not include a long-term mortgage obligation. However, the home is generally purchased below market value. To purchase a home by auction or foreclosed home, please visit http://www.newlyforeclosedhomes.com, or http://www.bankforeclosedlistings.com.

What Is A Foreclosure?
A foreclosed home is when the homeowner's ownership is terminated by default, because of his inability to make the mortgage payments. Once this happens, the home is sold by the lender; the bank, or whoever has legal ownership of the home at the time foreclosure occurs.

Other Ways To Invest In Your Home By Keeping It Affordable
Adjustable-Rate ARM Mortgage Bond
Helps guard against rising rates. When the mortgage rate rises, so does the payments of the ARM Mortgage Bond, which helps you to offset inflation.

What Is A Mortgage- Backed Security?
A Mortgage- Backed Security is an asset-backed security or debt obligation that represents a claim on the cash flows from mortgage loans through a process known as securitization.

Mortgage-Backed Bonds
A Mortgage-Backed Bond usually yields a high return based on interests, but requires high investment premiums to join.

Sources
U.S. Department of Housing and Urban Development
Federal Trade Commission
WikipediaThe Free Online Encyclopedia

Section Two
Home Sweet Home

This section covers the following topic:
Avoid Losing Your Home To Foreclosure

What Can I Do When I Am Behind In My Mortgage Payments?

The Federal Trade Commission says some homeowners who are struggling to make their mortgage payments may qualify for a modification loan under the Home Affordable Modification Program known as (HAMP).

What Is HAMP?

The Obama Administration introduced (HAMP) in 2009. The program was designed to help struggling homeowners save their homes by preventing foreclosure. The Home Affordable Modification Program gives homeowners a platform to refinance their mortgages, if their home has depreciated, or if the home has fallen below market value. In short, the program was implemented as a result of the 2008 subprime mortgage crisis/scandal of 2008; a time, in which America was on the brink of economic turmoil.

What Are The Eligibility Requirements To Receive HAMP Assistance?

*To qualify for the program, the home in question must be the primary residence.
*The amount, in which you owe, must be less than $729,750 on your first mortgage (primary residence).
*Your mortgage must have originated before January 1, 2009.
*Mortgage payments must be more than 31% of your current gross income, which includes the principal, interest, insurance, and etc.
To learn more, please visit http://www.ustreas.gov/press/releases/tg33.htm, or to request assistance, please visit http://my.barackobama.com or http://www.theobamahamp.com.

How Can I Avoid Defaulting On My Mortgage Loan?

FTC says homeowners should consider the following available plans:

What Is A Reinstatement Plan?

A reinvestment plan is when you pay the lender the entire past due amount, including late fees at a time, in which both you and the lender agrees. FTC says this plan usually works in temporary circumstances.

101

What Is A Repayment Plan?

A repayment plan is when the lender adds the past due amount to your existing mortgage payment. FTC says this option is good if someone has missed a few mortgage payments.

What Is A Forbearance?

A Forbearance enables borrowers to reduce or suspend mortgage payments for a set period of time. After the set time has expired, the borrower resumes regular scheduled mortgage payments, including paying one lump sum for the number of months payments were in deferment. The Federal Trade Commission says a forbearance might be the answer for those who have lost their job or whose income has been reduced.

What Is A Loan Modification?

A loan modification plan is when you and your lender agree to make permanent changes to the terms of your mortgage, as a way to make your mortgage payments more affordable.

How Can I Avoid Foreclosure?

FTC says borrowers should consider the following program options:

Short Sale

A short sale is when a lender allows the homeowner to sell the home before it goes into foreclosure. Thereby, agreeing to forgive any loss between the sale price and the mortgage balance. Many homeowners choose a short sale over foreclosure, because it can prove less damaging to your credit score.

An Important Note

"The Mortgage Forgiveness Debt Relief Act of 2007, HR 3648, protects homeowners from paying taxes on cancelled mortgage debt," as noted by Open Congress for the 112th United States Congress. For more information, please visit http://www.opencongress.org/bill/110-h3648/show ,or http://www.govtrack.us/congress/bill.xpd?bill=h110-3648.

Deed In Lieu of Foreclosure

A deed in lieu of foreclosure is when the lien holder agrees to have the property title transferred to the bank or to the lien holder, as a way to have the remainder of the debt on your home forgiven. However, a deed in lieu of foreclosure can adversely affect your Fico score, which is your credit score. Therefore, to avoid a negative credit rating, ask the lender to consider giving you an "unrated" credit score at the time that the deed in lieu is being negotiated, as it is less damaging to your credit score.

Sell Your Home

Selling your home is also doable when your lender postpones foreclosure proceedings, while you have a pending sales contract, or if you have placed your home on the market. FTC says "this approach works if proceeds from the sale covers the entire loan balance, plus expenses connected to selling the home (for example, real estate agent fees). In short, selling your home would not only help you avoid legal fees, it also protects your equity in the home.

Sources

Federal Trade Commission at http://www.ftc.gov
The White House government website at www.whitehouse.gov.
The non-profit Sunlight Foundation.
OpenCongress, a project by the Participatory Politics Foundation.

"The ideal man bears the accidents of life with dignity and grace, making the best of circumstances."

-President John F. Kennedy-

Photo: Public Domain Original author of photo Cecil Stoughton, White House   Photograph in the Oval Office July 11, 1963

104

Chapter Sixteen
A MAN'S HOME IS HIS CASTLE
(An American Proverb)

This chapter covers the following topic:
Purchasing A Home After Foreclosure

Can I Purchase A Home After Foreclosure?
Yes, you can purchase a home after foreclosure, according to Fannie Mae.

Who Is Fannie Mae?
Fannie Mae is America's largest mortgage buyer of conventional loans. In short, Fannie Mae sets loan amounts and requirements for borrowers.

What Is A Conventional Loan?
A conventional loan is a mortgage that is not guaranteed, nor is it insured by a government agency. This, includes the Federal Housing Administration, the Farmers Home Administration , and the Department of Veterans Affairs. Generally, conventional loans are a term of 30 years, with a fixed-interest rate.

For Conventional Loans Only!
Is There A Waiting Period To Purchase Another Home After Foreclosure?
Yes, the wait period is five years up to 7 years.

Can I Purchase A Home With No Extenuating Circumstances?
Yes, the wait period is four years from the date Deed-in-lieu of foreclosure was recorded.

Can I Purchase A Home After Foreclosure Having Extenuating Circumstances?
Yes, the wait period is three years up to 7 years.

Can I Purchase A Home After A Deed-in-Lieu of Foreclosure?
Yes, the wait period is four years up to 7 years.

Can I Purchase A Home After A Deed-in-Lieu of Foreclosure With Extenuating Circumstances?
Yes, the wait period is two years up to 7 years.

Can I Purchase A Home After A Short Sale?
Yes, the wait period is two years.

An Important Note
Guidelines mentioned above only apply to borrowers who submitted loan applications after August 1, 2008. Since October 2010, it is rumor that Fannie Mae may eventually change some policy options to make borrowers wait a mandatory seven years to purchase another home after foreclosure. Also, there maybe additional requirements added to secure a loan, as each mortgage loan varies. For additional information, please visit Fannie Mae at www.fanniemae.com , as policies are updated regularly.

Sources
Fannie Mae At www.fanniemae.com, or you can visit
Fannie Mae at
http://www.fanniemae.com/kb/index?page=home&c=search&startover=y&q=purchase+home+after+foreclosure.
Fannie Mae at
https://www.efanniemae.com/sf/guides/ssg/annltrs/pdf/2008/0816.pdf.
Fannie Mae Selling Guide: Underwriting Borrowers With a Prior Foreclosure at
https://www.efanniemae.com/sf/guides/ssg/annltrs/pdf/2010/sel1008.pdf.

"Education is the passport for the future, for tomorrow belongs to those who prepare for it."

- Malcolm X-

Chapter Seventeen
Common Sense Rules
(By Vladimir Nabokov <u>Russian</u> born <u>American</u>   <u>Novelist</u>, <u>Critic</u> and <u>Author</u> of "Lolita", <u>1899-1977</u>)

This chapter covers the following topics:

Paying Your Children's College Education The Smart Way

*UGMA-Uniform Gifts to Minors Act

*UTMA-Uniform Transfers to Minors Act

*529 College Plan

*U Promise College Plan

*Variable Annuities and Mutual Funds

*Veteran Benefits for Military Dependents

Uniform Gifts to Minors Act (UGMA) or the

Uniform Transfers to Minors Act (UTMA)/Custodial Plans

Under the Estate and Gift Tax Provision Act, the IRS offers a tax efficient way to give money and assets to minors, without having to consult an attorney, or pay costly legal fees. According to Sallie Mae, "the UGMA and the UTMA are the most tax efficient ways to save money for college and transfer wealth to your children and grandchildren."

What Is A UTMA Account?

The UTMA account allows you to transfer assets and real estate to minors.

What Is A UGMA Account?

The UGMA limits transfers and gifts to bank deposits, mutual funds insurance policies, and securities to minors. Sallie Mae explained that "UGMA and UTMA accounts are a way for children who are not of age of majority — younger than 18 in most states and 21 in others — to own securities (stocks, mutual funds, bonds, etc.)."

How Can I Set Up A UGMA/UTMA Account?

You can set up a UGMA/UTMA account by visiting your local bank, broker, or mutual fund manager.

What Is The Procedure In Setting Up A UGMA/UTMA Account?

You will need the { Name of Custodian} as custodian for Name of Minor}, and under The Uniform Gifts to Minors Act {Name of State of Minor's residence}. The minor's Social Security number is used as the taxpayer's identification on the account. Although monies officially belong to the minor, the custodian has legal fiduciary over the account. Meaning, the custodian is responsible for handling the account in a "prudent manner" on behalf of the minor.

According to federal guidelines, the custodian can invest in common stocks, but cannot write naked options. (Once the minor becomes of legal age, 18 or 21, depending on which state he or she resides, the donor and/or custodian of the account no longer has any control over it, and the child is free to spend the money as he or she chooses.

An Important Note

To my understanding, although UGMA/UTMA accounts are considered custodial accounts, in which parents set up for their minor children, it is not always in the best interest of the parent to act as the custodian of the account, as income from the account is generally taxed to the parent. However, if the parent is both the donor and custodian of the account, and dies before the minor child becomes of legal age to take over the account, the income from the UGMA/UTMA is generally placed in the custodian's estate and thereby, protected and given over to the child when he or she reaches legal age. **For additional information,** please visit the RIA Federal Tax Coordinator 2d, volume 22A, paragraph R-2619, which states "Giving cash, stocks, bonds, notes, etc., to children through a custodian may result in the transferred property being included in the donor's gross estate unless someone other than the donor is named as custodian." Please see Lober, Louis v. US, 346 US 335 (1953) (53-2 USTC par. 10922); Rev Ruls 57-366, 59-357, 70-348 to see why it is not good for the parent to be both donor and custodian on the account.

Tax Filing And Implications

The custodian submits a W-9 Form to IRS.
According to Sallie Mae:

- "UGMA/UTMA is subject to the $12,000 Gift Tax Exclusion that allows an individual to give up to $12,000 per year to another person without being subjected to the Gift Tax.
- The first $850 in earnings each year is free from federal taxes and the next $850 is taxed at the child's tax rate. Afterwards, earnings are taxed at the normal rates.
- UGMA/UTMA accounts can be rolled over into 529 plans, which is a very common occurrence considering the more generous tax benefits and account ownership flexibility."

Source
Sallie Mae at
https://www1.salliemae.com/before_college/parents_plan/ways_to_pay/saving/gifts_transfer.htm or visit
http://www.collegeanswer.com/paying/content/ugma_utma.jsp
The IRS at www.irs.gov/pub/irs-pdf/fw9.pdf.
U.S. Department of the Treasury at
http://www.treasury.gov/Pages/Search.aspx?k=(scope%3a%22allsites%22)+ALL(The+Uniform+Gifts+to+Minors+Act).

Section Two
Common Sense Rules

What Is A Section II 529 College Savings Plan?
It is considered an educational savings plan operated by a state or educational entity, which enables families to set aside money for future college expenses and tuition. Please see Section 529 of the Internal Revenue Code,[1] 26 U.S.C. § 529 (since 1996).

Does The 529 College Savings Plan Leave Room For Flexibility?
Yes. The 529 College Plan works much like a 401K or IRA, if you invest your contributions in a mutual fund. In short, the plan offers several investment options, in which you can choose at will. To date, all states offer the 529 College Savings Plan.

Prepaid Plans
With a prepaid plan, you can pay all, or part of the costs of an in-state public college education. Prepaid plans may also be converted for use at private and out-of-state colleges. The Independent 529 Plan is a separate

prepaid plan for private colleges. To view benefits of establishing a Private College 529 Plan, which range from paying less college tuition to receiving tax advantages, please visit https://www.privatecollege529.com/OFI529/PN/generated/en_us/Primary Navigation_03-26-10-092753.xml.

Who Has Control Over The Account?

"*The donor controls the account

*Beneficiary has no rights to the funds.

*Donor decides when withdrawals are taken and for what purpose.

*Usually, plans allow you to reclaim the funds for yourself any time you desire, no questions asked. (However, the earnings portion of the "non-qualified" withdrawal will be subject to income tax and an additional 10% penalty tax)."

How Can I Set Up A 529 College Plan?

* Visit your local bank and simply request an enrollment form.

* Make a contribution.

* You have the option of setting up the account direct deposit.

*Generally, plan assets are handled by the state treasurer's office, or an outside investment company hired as the actor/ program manager. To learn more, please visit https://www.privatecollege529.com or call 1-888-718-7878.

Eligibility

*Anyone can invest in a 529 College Savings Plan.

* You are allowed to make contributions in large amounts.

* No income limitations or age restrictions noted for contributors: Parents, grandchildren, relatives can make a contribution.

Federal Tax Benefit

The tax-free treatment was made permanent with the Pension Protection Act of 2006.

*Your investment grows tax-deferred, although contributions are not tax deductible.

* You are not required to file Form 1099, until you make a withdrawal.

An Important Note

The 529 College Savings Plan can affect your financial aid award amount, according to FAFSA. In short, the plan affects the student's Expected

Family Contribution (EFC), which is considered a parental asset.

Upromise
What Is A Upromise College Fund?
Upromise, Inc. is headquartered in Newton, Massachusetts . It is an American corporation that was launched in April 2001. Upromise is one of the largest, private sources of college funding in the United States.
You can request a Upromise membership at http://www.upromise.com, or at https://lty.s.upromise.com/secure/login.do.

Upromise-How Does It Work?
Upromise allows "Members to receive contributions when making everyday purchases of products and services at more than 21,000 grocery and drug stores, 14,000 gas stations, and 8,000 restaurants, as well as thousands of retail stores and more than 600 online shopping sites." In addition, Upromise college savings rewards can be applied to student loan debt. In August 2006, Upromise was recognized by Sallie Mae. The "529" college savings plans are offered through Upromise Investments, Inc. (member FINRA/SIPC), with investment management by The Vanguard Group."

An Important Note
Upromise partners include, "CVS/pharmacy, Citicorp, ExxonMobil Corporation, Bed Bath & Beyond, McDonalds, JCPenney, LandsEnd, Sears, iTunes, and hundreds of others," as provided by Wikipedia The Online Encyclopedia.

Sources
U.S. Securities and Exchange Commission
U.S. Department of the Treasury
Saving for college at http://www.savingforcollege.com.
Wikipedia, The Online Encyclopedia at http://en.wikipedia.org/wiki/Upromise.

United States Department Of Veteran Affairs: College Benefits For Dependent Children Of Military Servicemembers
Survivors' and Dependents' Educational Assistance Program (DEA)
According to the Department of Veteran Affairs, "Dependents' Educational Assistance provides education and training opportunities to

veterans' dependents who are eligible for the program.
*Offers up to 45 months of educational benefits.
*Dependent children can use benefits for a degree or certificate
program and/or apprenticeship, or on-the-job training programs.

What Are The Eligibility Requirements To Receive Benefits?
"You must be the son, daughter, or spouse of a veteran who died or is
permanently and totally disabled, as the result of a service-connected
disability. The disability must arise out of active service in the Armed
Forces.

- A veteran who died from any cause while such service-connected
  disability was in existence. Also, a service member missing in
  action or captured in line of duty by a hostile force.
- A service member forcibly detained or interned in line of duty by a
  foreign government or power.
- A service member who is hospitalized or receiving outpatient
  treatment for a service connected permanent and total disability
  and is likely to be discharged for that disability."

An Important Note
The following changes were made effective December 23, 2006:
"If you are a son or daughter and wish to receive benefits for attending
school or job training, you must be between the ages of 18 and 26. In
certain instances, it is possible to begin before age 18 and to continue after
age 26. Marriage is not a bar to this benefit. If you are in the Armed
Forces, you may not receive this benefit while on active duty. To pursue
training after military service, your discharge must not be under
dishonorable conditions. VA can extend your period of eligibility by the
number of months and days equal to the time spent on active duty. This
extension cannot generally go beyond your 31st birthday, there are some
exceptions," according to the Department of Veteran Affairs.

How Can I Apply For Benefits?
You can request VA Form 22-5490, which is an application for Survivors'
and Dependents' Educational Assistance located at
http://www.osfa.uiuc.edu/forms/1011/AEBDEA.pdf, or you can reference

the Survivors' and Dependents' Educational Assistance Program -Pamphlet. For additional inquiries, you can contact your local VA Regional Office toll-free at 1-888-442-4551.

Source
http://www.gibill.va.gov/pamphlets/CH35/CH35_Pamphlet_General.htm, please visit the U.S. Department of Veterans Affairs site to learn more about educational benefits for dependent children.

How Can I Help Pay My Child's College Education With An Annuity?
*If your child is older than 10 years old, you can open a variable annuity for him, or you can consider investing in an Education Annuity Trust.
*The account must be open in your name (the Adult), but making the child the beneficiary. For more information, please visit http://www.si-giftlegacy.com/giftlaw/glawpro_subsection.jsp?WebID=GL2005-0877&CC=3&SS=1&SS2=9#Link1.

How Can I Help Pay For My Child's College Education With Mutual Funds?
*Children under ten, can open a separate brokerage account in your name (the adult), while you invest money in a growth fund through an Index Fund or Exchange Traded Fund. To learn more, please visit the following: www.finaid.org, www.collegeboard.com, or www.NASFAA.org.

Section Three
Common Sense Rules

What Options Do I Have As A College Student Who Is Economically Disadvantaged Or Homeless?

A Online and Reference Guide for College Students
The SAT Program Fee-Waiver Service
http://sat.collegeboard.com/register/sat-fee-waivers

U.S. Department Of Health Human Services For Grants And Scholarships
http://www.hhs.gov, or visit http://www.hhs.gov/grants.

Search Various Scholarships Offered
http://bhpr.hrsa.gov/dsa/sds.htm
http://www.hhs.gov/grants

Scholarships Disadvantaged Students
http://www.hrsa.gov/loanscholarships/index.html
Loans And Scholarships For Students In Health Science Fields
http://bhpr.hrsa.gov/dsa/lds.htm

College Grants
http://www.grantstudy.gov

Health Professions Student Loans For Disadvantaged Students
http://bhpr.hrsa.gov/dsa/hpsl.htm

The National Health Service Corps
http://nhsc.hrsa.gov
Receive tuition, fees, stipend for cost-of-living for up to 4 years

Jobs For Indians And Alaska Natives
http://www.ihs.gov/index.cfm?module=Jobs

Personal Grant Funding
http://www.benefits.gov

Federal Student Aid
http://studentaid.ed.gov/PORTALSWebApp/students/english/index.jsp

Help For Students With Children
http://www.hhs.gov/children/index.html

Child Care Assistance And Referral Agency Programs
http://nccic.acf.hhs.gov/emergency/topic_childcare.cfm

Child Care Awareness Program
Help Pay Child Care Expenses
http://www.childcareaware.org/docs/pubs/110e.pdf

College Students AT- Risk Recovery Assistance
Apply For Food Stamps While You Attend College
Apply at the Department Of Health And Human Services in your state. To learn about how it works, please visit
http://www.masslegalhelp.org/income-benefits/food-stamps/college

Sign-Up For SHARE - A National Food Share Program
http://www.sharedc.org, or call 1-800-21-SHARE

Search The National Database For Emergency Assistance
http://www.ampleharvest.org/211.php?gclid=CMLNnLGn_qQCFQ915Qod1QUAjw
or call 1-877-652-1148.

Search The National Directory For Homeless Shelters
http://www.homelessshelterdirectory.org/washingtondc.html

Search Homeless Shelter Directory/ Soup Kitchens /Food Pantries
http://www.homelessshelterdirectory.org/cgi-
bin/id/cityfoodbanks.cgi?city=Washington&state=DC

Students Who Are Homeless -Find Shelter And Monetary Assistance
 http://www.naehcy.org/resources.html, or visit
http://www.naehcy.org/letendre_app.html to apply for a scholarship or

download an application.

Mail Packets To:

Patricia A. Popp, Ph.D.

The LeTendre Education Fund

The National Association for the Education of Homeless Children and Youth

9176 Harvey Hollow Drive

Mechanicsville, Virginia 23116, or fax it to 757-221-5300.

Federal Assisted Programs

U.S. Department of Health Human Services

http://www.hhs.gov/homeless

U.S. Department Of Veteran Affairs

http://www1.va.gov/homeless

U.S. Department of Labor

http://www.dol.gov/dol/audience/aud-homeless.htm

U.S. Department Of Agriculture

Nutrition Assistance Programs

http://www.fns.usda.gov/fns

U.S. Department Of Education

http://www2.ed.gov/programs/homeless/index.html

Other Homeless Assistance Programs

National Association For The Education Of Homeless Children And Youth

www.naehcy.org

National Center For Homeless Education

www.serve.org/nche

National Center For Homelessness Education
www.serve.org/nche

National College Access Network
www.collegeaccess.org

Covenant House
http://www.covenanthouse.org

A National directory For College Students And Youth
http://www.nationalhomeless.org/directories/directory_national.pdf

Search Programs By State
http://www.hudhre.info

Homeless Emergency And Rapid Transition To Housing Act Of 2009
http://www.hudhre.info/hearth

The Homelessness Prevention Fund and Rapid Re-Housing Program
http://www.hudhre.info/HPRP

The National Run Away Switchboard
http://www.nrscrisisline.org, or call 1-800-786-2929

Assistance For Homeless Youth And Transitional Housing
http://homelessyouthamongus.org

Search The National Homeless Shelter Database
http://www.shelterlistings.org/find_shelter.html

Search For Housing Grants

http://www.mygovernmentresources.com/housing_grants.html?campaign=9927
74l&adgroup=290300961&keyword=housing%20grants&type=search&engine=G
&gclid=COGhpfadgKUCFVB95QodVDwNig.

Chapter Eighteen
AMERICAN AS APPLE PIE
(An American Proverb)

This chapter covers the following topic:

Tax Burdens Made Easy Through Investing

Dreading that time of year again, the time of year when everyone is rushing to see the tax preparer, in order to avoid paying late fines, fees, or any other penalties that the government can impose on you , if you fail to file your federal taxes on time? I found, the best way to avoid stressing at tax time is prepare for tax time early. I have come to realize over the years that if you invest smart, tax time can be beneficial to both you and Uncle Sam.

As a former tax preparer for H&R Block, and through personal experiences, I found investing in tax-deferred stocks and bonds, and other money markets can be beneficial to you, especially at tax time. Instead of stressing over taxes this year, learn ways you can invest your money throughout the year and possibly earn more cash. Then, when it comes time to pay Uncle Sam, you will be happy to do so, because you peaceful knowing that you got your cut first. Listen! view the options below, and see which investments might work best for you.

Softening The Impact Of Tax Burdens Through Investing

Invest in the following:
*401 (K) Retirement Savings Plan
*403 (b), which is offered by nonprofit organizations
*Roth 401 (k) Plans
*Annuities
*U.S. Security Bonds
*Keogh Plan

An Important Note

The plans mentioned above are tax-deferred. Meaning, you can save money towards your retirement, without having to pay taxes on it. However, at the time of withdrawal, taxes become due. Also, IRAs and

Keogh plans are tax-deferred, such as in dividends, capital gains, and interests. Roth IRAs are not tax deductible.

What Is A 401 (K) Plan?
Established by employers for retirees
*Income accrues on a tax-deferred basis.
*You can borrow from it before you retire. However, a penalty may apply for early withdrawals. In some cases and with good reason, penalties may be waived in certain circumstances, such as purchasing a home or going back or to college. Each plan is different, so make sure you choose a plan that is most suitable for you.

What Is A 403 (b) Nonprofit Retirement Plan?
*the plan provides steady income at a predetermined amount when you retire.
*Plan is popular, because it does not require an employer contribution.

What Is A Roth 401 (K) Plan?
*Income tax paid or either withheld during the year of contributions.
*Distributions and Income that accrue from the plan are tax free.

What Are Annuities?
*Provide income for you after you retire, but taxed when you withdraw or start to withdraw money from it.
*A fixed Annuity can yield you a fixed payment amount.
*It is a safe, but low yielding investment.

What Are U.S. Security Bonds?
Securities are United States Treasury bills, notes, and bonds.
*Bonds are debts paid to you by the U.S. Government (a guarantee).
* Bonds have a market liquidity in (business, economics, and investments).
*Money and cash on hand is perhaps, its best asset.
*Heavily Traded
*It is known as a safe investment to make since it is backed by the government.

What Is A Keogh Plan?
It is a retirement plan for the self-employed and small business.
There are two types of plans:
* Defined-benefit, which is a fixed contribution and defined-contribution, which is considered a more complex plan.

*The Keogh Plan has a high contribution rate.
* "Employees can generally contribute up to $16,500 per year, and the employer can contribute up to $49,000, for a total annual contribution of $65,500 (www.irs.gov/pub/irs-pdf/p560.pdf)," as noted by Wikipedia The Free Encyclopedia.

What Are Other Investments That Yield You Cash At Retirement?
Balanced Fund
*Yields you current income,
 usually not for commercial investors.

Municipal Bond
*Provides you tax-free income

Single State Fund
*The money you save is free from federal and state taxation.
*The Fund is considered tax-free income.
*Usually, the Fund provides a high return.

International Bond Fund
* Provides you income.
*Allows you diversification.
*Guards against the depreciation on the dollar.

Short Term Bonds Fund
*Matures in 2 to 5 years.
*Yields you income with limited risk.

Intermediate-Term Bond Funds
A good investment for a young person.
*Yields a steady source of income, but does not mature for 15 to 30 years.

An Important Note
 Avoid purchasing high yield bonds, which are considered "Junk Bonds."

Aggressive Growth Funds
*Maximizes Capital Gains.
*Growth Funds are good for inflation on the dollar.
*Usually, with Growth Funds, earnings increase steadily.

What Are Growth & Income Funds?
*It pays significant dividend income.
*However, cost increases with your current income.

What Are Income Funds?
*Provides current income, however, in the long-run the price increases.

What Are Mortgage -Backed Bonds?
"Is an asset-backed security or debt obligation that represents a claim on the cash flows from mortgage loans through a process known as securitization," as defined by Wikipedia The Online Encyclopedia.
*Generally, the bond is issued by The Government National Mortgage Association.

What Are Adjustable-Rate Mortgage Bonds?
*The bonds help to guard against rising rates.
*As mortgage rate rises, mortgage bonds increase payments.
*Pays a low yield

How Does Equity Fund Investors Make Money?
Investors make money from the following:
*Dividends
*Capital Gains
*Share Price Appreciation

An Important Note
There are more investment options available to you, however, I found these investments to be most useful in improving debt situations. If you are looking to ease your tax burdens and earn additional income, check with your local bank and investment brokers to see what other investments might be suitable for you.

Although Irene is a former tax preparer for H& R Block, Irene is not a banker, an investment broker or an expert in money markets. She is just like you, an average American citizen desiring to invest smart and be able to retire without having to worry about how she is going to live in her golden years.

A Major Tax Nugget
Those who are at risk in having their tax refund intercepted by the IRS due

to delinquent child support payments or due to federal debt, consider filing a Married, but Filing Separate Injured Spouse Claim.

How Is Injured Spouse Defined?
An injured spouse pertains to a debt that your spouse incurred before you got married, in which you have no legal obligation to repay.

Why File A Married Filing Separate Injured Spouse Claim?
When the federal and state governments have the legal right to intercept or take a tax refund due to the non-custodial parent delinquency in child support payments or federal debt. You can file "FORM 8379" with the U.S. Department of the Treasury Internal Revenue Service at http://www.irs.gov/pub/irs-pdf/f8379.pdf.

What Are The Benefits of Filing An Injured Spouse Claim?
The innocent spouse who does not owe any back child support or federal debt will not have his or her tax return intercepted by the IRS. However, the spouse who owes the debt is still obligated to pay arrears and still remains in danger of having his or her tax return intercepted by the IRS.

Who Is Eligible To File An Injured Spouse Claim?
When you are not legally obligated to pay a delinquent federal debt, such as a student loan, foreclosures, and any other federal debts," as explained by the Internal Revenue Service.

What Are The Benefit of Filing An Injured Spouse Claim?
If you, the innocent spouse, learn that your tax return can be intercepted by the IRS due to your spouse's delinquency in paying back a federal debt, you can contact the IRS and request "An Injured Spouse Form) so, you will not be penalized by the IRS and therefore, receive your tax return without incident.

When Can I File An Injured Spouse Claim?
Usually, you can file Form 8379, which is an injured spouse claim at the end of the year when you file your taxes. However, talk to your tax preparer and ask questions. If you need further assistance, please contact the IRS at http://www.irs.gov/localcontacts/index.html.

How Does It Work?
Simply have your tax preparer attach Form 8379 to your tax return and mail it to the IRS.

Sources
Board of Governors of the Federal Reserve System
http://www.federalreserve.gov.
Federal Reserve Board: Consumer Information
www.federalreserve.gov/consumers.htm.
Federal Reserve Education
http://www.federalreserveeducation.org.
The Internal Revenue Service
http://www.irs.gov.
The Internal Revenue Service for Recognition of Exemption
http://www.irs.gov/charities/article/0,,id=96109,00.html.
Merriam-Webster Dictionary
http://www.learnersdictionary.com/search/capitalism.
Wikipedia, The Free Encyclopedia at
http://en.wikipedia.org/wiki/Taxation_in_the_United_States.

Sources
Forbes 2010 Mutual Fund Guide Investment Company Institute (The National Association of U.S. Investment Companies), Fidelity.com, Vanguard, Mass Mutual Financial Group, Money And Markets by Nilus Mattive 02-09-10, and U.S. Securities and Exchange Commission.
Wikipedia The Online Free Encyclopedia.

"I do not think much of a man who is not wiser today than he was yesterday. My great concern is not whether you have failed, but whether you are content with your failure."
(Photo: Public Domain)

-Abraham Lincoln-

Chapter Nineteen
SEED TIME And HARVEST
(Genesis 8:22 KJV)

This chapter covers the following topic:
Investments That Yield You Cash

In the past, studies revealed Americans earned more money between ages 36 - 60, however, today this is no longer true. According to a 2008 study titled, "Average Lifetime Earnings By Education Trajectories," conducted by the U.S. Census Bureau, covering periods 1998-2008, revealed a person's income generally rose from ages 50-54 and after age 54, dropped off in earned income levels. Also, the study revealed in 1997-2007, the average starting income for person's ages 18-24 ranged from $21, 834 - $35, 903, depending on the person's education level: the lower wage earner having less than a high school education and the higher wage earner earning up to a Bachelor's degree.

After taking into consideration the study's findings, what troubled me the most about the outcome of income trajectories is that over the years, Americans have become better educated and are making more money now than ever before, which brings me to ask this question, "why are most Americans still broke?" Perhaps, the answer lies in the absence of Americans being taught about the principles of money and investing earlier on in life, such as in junior high school, or at the high school level. I mean, what is the point in getting a basic education, if it does not include the bottom line: money.

This chapter is intended to educate and persuade young people to invest and save early, as they set out to establish their careers and make major financial decisions. Listed below are a few of the many investments you can make, including items that you can add in order to help you build a healthy financial portfolio.

What Are Fixed-Rate Capital Securities?
*It is a security issued by a corporation at a par value of $25.

*It offers investors a combination of corporate bonds and/or preferred stock.
 *It offers a fixed-monthly income (quarterly or semiannual income), as well as offers an attractive yield.
* Fixed-Rate Securities are fairly liquid, and is generally rated as a credit quality investment.
*Fixed-Rate Securities is a long-term investment, with a maturity date**.**

What Is A Money Market Checking And Savings Account?
*It is a high-interest Savings Account that offers a competitive interest rate. In short, you earn higher dividends, if you can keep your account balance on the high-end.
*It combines your checking and savings. You can save and spend money at the same time.
*You can withdraw money by check, or you can have money transferred into your Savings Account.

What Is A Money Market Fund?
*A Money Market Fund is an investment strategy having a larger return than the basic Savings Account. Also, some Money Market Mutual Funds are tax-exempt, and usually free from federal, state, and city taxation. *Money Market accounts generally offer stable income.

What Is AAA Related Insured Municipal Bonds?
*AAA Related Insured Municipal Bonds offers the insured interest income. Bonds offer both short-term and long-term options: a short-term bond matures in one year, or less; and a long-term bond maturing after one year.
*Bonds are exempt from federal and state income taxes. Bonds ensure timely, scheduled principal interest payments. Bonds provide interest and capital repayments if the issuer defaults in payment. With AAA Bonds, if a company goes bankrupt or goes out-of-business a person's investments are still protected.

What Are Treasury Securities?
*Treasury Securities or fixed-income securities are U.S. debt obligations that are backed by the government. There are three types of securities: bills, bonds, and notes. By purchasing Treasury

Securities, you are loaning money to the government to meet its debt obligations. *Treasury Securities are exempt from federal and state taxation. However, federal taxes are expected on earned interest.*They are liquid and generally traded in secondary markets. *Although securities are a safe investment, they generally offer a low yield.

What Are Inflation –Indexed Securities?
*Inflation-Indexed Securities are inflation- protected securities. *Securities guarantee a return higher than the rate of inflation. *They protect investors against rising inflation. It generally pays interest twice a year, and at a fixed rate. *Interest payments rise when inflation is present, but pay decreases when inflation is absent.*Through an Inflation-Indexed Security Fund, you protect your retirement income from yearly inflation.

What Is Variable Universal Life Insurance?
*Variable Universal Life Insurance is like whole life insurance in that it builds cash value. *This insurance offers death benefits, and allows you to invest in various investment portfolios. *The premium amount is flexible and can be changed by you at anytime. *Variable Universal Life Insurance is considered a good retirement vehicle for earning extra cash.

What Is Zero Coupon Treasury Bonds?
*Zero Bonds are backed by the U.S. government. However, this is the only Security Treasury Bond that does not make scheduled interest payments. Zero Coupon Treasury Bonds pay a lump-sum interest payment only at the time of maturity (generally a Two-25 year investment). *Zero Coupon Treasury Bonds are sold at a discounted rate and at maturity; it pays you full face -value.

How Can I Prepare For My Retirement And Receive More Residual Income?
You can receive additional income by investing in a pre-tax retirement plan, such as the 401(K) Retirement Plan, or the 403(B) Retirement Plan, which is offered by nonprofits.

What Is An Annuity?
*Annuities provide a steady cash flow for individuals during

retirement. *Annuities are tax-deferred, until the point of withdrawal. *A Fixed Annuity guarantees a specific payout amount. *Annuities pay death benefits.

What Is A Charitable Remainder Annuity Trust?
*It is a popular life-income plan.   It is when cash, real property, securities, and various assets are transferred into a trust, and whoever manages the trust pays you a fixed income for a period of up to life. Also, you can leave money to beneficiaries.

What Is A SEP-IRA?
*SEP-IRA, which stands for Simplified Employee Pension Individual Retirement Account was created for self-employed persons. It is a retirement plan established by employers (sole proprietorships or partnerships), which offers retirement benefits to business owners and their employees. *Employers can make tax-deductible contributions, and employees do not have to pay taxes on their contributions, until the point of withdrawal.

What Is A Keogh Plan?
*A Keogh plan is a tax-deferred retirement plan offered to self-employed persons, or to companies that have not been incorporated. *With the Keogh Plan, contributions are tax-deductible up to 25% of your annual income, which is a lot higher than your basic Simplified Employee Pension Plan. *The value of the principal is also adjusted to equal inflation.

What Is An Individual Retirement Account (IRA)?
*An IRA, which is an Individual Retirement Account, is nothing more than a retirement savings plan that allows you to make limited contributions towards your retirement each year.
*Interest earned is tax-deferred. However, contributions are not tax deductible.

What Is A Roth IRA?
*A Roth IRA allows you to contribute more to the fund each month, which enables you to save more money towards your retirement. *Roth IRAs are not tax deductible, but money earned from interest is tax-free growth. *If you started investing late or started saving towards your retirement late, the Roth IRA maybe the solution for you, as it allows you to play catch-up.

What Is A Retirement CD?
*A Retirement CD is a time deposit promissory note, which is issued by a bank. It is similar to a Savings account.
*A Certificate of Deposit is FDIC and NCUA secured.
 *Yields are the result of accrued interest.
*Money can be withdrawn, with accrued interest at the time of maturity.

Sources
The U.S. Census bureau
U.S. Census' Current Population Survey: Average Lifetime Earnings Trajectories by Education at http://politicalcalculations.blogspot.com/2009/07/average-lifetime-earnings-trajectories.html and learn more about peak earnings.
Investopedia at http://www.investopedia.com.
Merrill Lynch Wealth Management Federal Deposit Insurance Corporation

"The ultimate measure of a man is not where he stands in moments of comfort and convenience, but where he stands at times of challenge and controversy."   -Dr. Martin Luther King, Jr.-

Photo: Public Domain. Dr. Martin Luther King Jr. March 26, 1964 Suggested credit: Trikosko/Library of Congress.

Chapter Twenty
It Ain't Over Until The Fat Lady Sings
(Originally a southern proverb, but attributed to writer/broadcaster Dan Cook)

This chapter covers the following topic:
What To Do When You've Hit Rock Bottom?
The U.S. Department of Housing and Urban Development defines homelessness as "homeless individuals and families who are sleeping in places not meant for human habitation, such as cars, parks, sidewalks, and abandoned buildings or those who are sleeping in an emergency shelter as a primary nighttime residence."

A List Of Agencies That Can Assist You In YourTime Of Need
The National Registry For Single Dad's Program
http://www.Helpfordads.org
*Rent and housing assistance
*Child care and food assistance
*Single father grants
*Utility bill assistance
*College tuition assistance
*Transportation assistance
Download a grant application at
http://helpfordads.org/Registration.html

Single Mother Assistance Program
http://singlemotherhelp.org
*Rent/housing assistance
*Utility bill assistance
*Child care assistance
*Food assistance
*College scholarship assistance
*Apply for a $10,000 scholarship at Scholarships4Moms.net
Download an application at
http://singlemotherhelp.org/single-mother-help-registration.php, or call 1-888-774-7282

USA Cares Program (A Post-911 Program)
For service members, veterans, and family members
*Rent and mortgage assistance

*Utility assistance
*Education and childcare assistance
*Transportation assistance
*Childcare and food assistance
*Vehicle repair
*Stress, brain, and injuries

You can download an application at
https://app.etapestry.com/hosted/USACaresInc/OnlineApplication.html

The Homeless Assistance Program (HUD)
http://www.hud.gov/subscribe/signup.cfm?listname=Homeless%20Assista
nce%20Program&list=HOMELESS-ASST-L.

The Supportive Housing Program
*Provides a means for private nonprofits, states, and local governments
to develop housing and services for homeless persons.
http://www.hud.gov/offices/cpd/homeless/programs/shp.

The Shelter Plus Care Program
*Provides rental assistance for homeless persons with disabilities.
*The Shelter Plus Care Program (S+C) offers long-term assistance for
homeless persons with disabilities and serious mental disabilities.
http://www.hud.gov/offices/cpd/homeless/programs/shp.

The Single Room Occupancy Program
*Provides rental assistance for homeless persons needing rehabilitation
assistance.
http://www.hud.gov/offices/cpd/homeless/programs/sro/index.cfm.

Emergency Shelter Grants Program
*Provides shelter and supportive services for homeless persons.
http://www.hud.gov/offices/cpd/homeless/programs/esg.

The Base Realignment And Closure Program
*Military property is transitioned to civilians. The program provides
priority care for homeless persons.
http://www.hud.gov/offices/cpd/homeless/programs/brac.

The Title V Program
*Falls under the McKinney-Vento Act. which allows the transfer of
federal properties to nonprofits, states, and local governments in order to

assist homeless persons.
http://www.hud.gov/offices/cpd/homeless/programs/t5.

Housing Opportunities For Persons Living With HIV
*Provides housing assistance for persons with HIV/AIDS.
http://www.hud.gov/offices/cpd/aidshousing/programs/index.cfm.

Homeless Veterans can call 1-877- 424-3838 for assistance
To learn more about homelessness in the United States, please visit
http://portal.hud.gov/portal/page/portal/HUD/topics/homelessness.

What Can I Do To Help Myself When I Am Down And Out?
*Draw unemployment if you are eligible.
*Contact your local area food bank.
* Contact your local area homeless shelter.
*Contact a neighborhood church and request any available assistance.
* Contact the American Red Cross.
* Contact the Salvation Army.
* Contact your community support center in your area.
*Apply for emergency food stamps at The Department of Health and
Human Services.
*Apply for the Homelessness to Homeownership Program
 through Habitat for Humanity.
*If you are homeless, try to find a job that offers "A room for
 work" option. Also, consider going back to college, or apply for a
degree-program and live on campus to off-set homelessness.

Desperate Times Cause For Desperate Measures
Irene's Emergency-Care Tips
*If you ever become homeless and you do not know what to do, go to a
24- hour restaurant, order coffee, study or read a book until morning.
*If you are homeless, go to a bus station, stay for a couple of hours,
regroup and call the emergency shelter unit for assistance. Also, if the
station allows you to stay over night, do so. Then, the next day continue to
search for shelter.
*If a bus station or emergency shelter is not available, stay in your car
overnight in a well, lit, low-crime area, such as (an apartment complex, a
24-hour restaurant, a 24-hour grocery store, or a 7-Eleven store, until you
can find shelter).
*Enroll in the Job Core Program.

*For quick cash, visit your local area Pond Shop and sell
any items of any value.
*Consider applying for a cash advance loan, but only as a last resort.
*Work in the field: pick blue berries, grapes, cherries, and etc
 to earn money.
*Sell your car to the auto-auction.

An Important Note
Park your car in a busy downtown area on the side of the street
where there is a big event taking place. Wait until the parking garage near
the event is full, and then make an offer to someone looking for a parking
space. For example, "I will move my car so you can park here for less
than what it would cost you to pay a parking garage." Believe me, this
really works.

How Can I Save On My Grocery Bill?
You will never spend a ridiculous price on groceries again.
*Register with Grocery Coupon Network at
gcn.newsletter@grocerycouponnetwork.com and receive nationwide
name-brand food coupons.
*Register with CouponCabin.com to receive name-brand coupons for
nonperishable items, such as Lane Bryant, Toys R Us, Target, Kohls, and
etc. Also, learn alternative ways, in which you can contribute to America's
food supply by making the most of your home, yard, or land.

Plant A Vegetable Garden
Grow onions, potatoes, cabbage,
collard greens, beans, tomatoes, peppers, and etc.

 Plant Fruit Trees In Your Yard
*Plant an apple tree, a pear tree, a cherry tree, an orange tree, and, etc.
*Cities and states can assist in developing community gardens to
 help feed America's needy families in neighborhoods throughout the
country.
*Individuals with large families
*should consider cooking home-made dishes that are filling, but
inexpensive. Consider stocking up on the following items:
*Purchase flour and corn meal to bake your own bread
*Purchase beans and rice for dishes that are filling
*Go fishing and have a fish fry.

*Hunt wild game, such as deer, rabbit, and etc.
*Prepare meals that you can serve again as leftovers
*Consider grilling outside on a regular basis. You can save on your gas and electric bill by grilling your meats, vegetables outside on the grill.

Irene's ReusableTips
*Refill empty perfume bottle with water (half way) in order to use up any leftover cologne residue. This also works for bubble bath , shampoo, and any other household cleaning items.
*If you wear post earrings and lose the stud to an earring, you can replace the stud with a small piece of sponge, or a rubbery substance to hold the earring in place.
*If you have a corn on your toe, you can use your facial makeup to cover it up (my cosmetic fix).

How To Give Gifts On Birthdays And Holidays When I'm Short On Cash?
*Register for free birthday gifts at
http://thebirthdayregister.com/selectyourgifts.asp.
*Register for Birthday freebies and gift certificates, and free meals at
http://www.heyitsfree.net/2006/10/03/birthday-freebies.
*Register with Birthday e-Cards at
http://www.123greetings.com/birthday/gifts.
* Register with Hallmark and send someone you love a free 'e-Card' at
http://www.hallmark.com/online.
*Register for free Christmas gifts at
http://www.christmasfreebies.com/freechristmasgifts.html.
*Register with Toys for Tots and receive free gifts at
http://www.toysfortots.org, or inquire about free Christmas gifts for children at The Salvation Army.
*Register for free gifts at http://www.thefreesite.com.

Chapter Twenty-One
The Pursuit of Happiness
(The United States Declaration of Independence)

This chapter covers the following topic:
Life Insurance Policies That Yield You Cash

The Affordable Care Act Tax Provisions
Enacted March 23, 2010

The Act allows young adults to stay on their parents' health care plan, until they reach age 26. Starting 2011, the Act requires "employers to report the value of health insurance coverage they provide employees on each employee's annual Form W-2," as noted by the Internal Revenue Service." **To view other benefits offered under the Affordable Care Act Tax Provisions,** such as the Small Business Health Care Tax Credit, the Adoption Credit, the Medicare Part D Coverage , and Gap Rebate, please visit the IRS at www.irs.gov/newsroom/article/0,,id=220809,00.html.

What Is Term Life Insurance?

Term Life Insurance provides coverage for a limited period of time and usually, at a fixed rate. Term Life Insurance is one of the most affordable ways to acquire death benefits. Also, it pays face value amount of the insurance policy to the beneficiary. In short, you can purchase Term Life Insurance for one year up to 30 years.

What Is Level Term Life Insurance?

Level Term Life Insurance provides coverage at a fixed-rate for a limited period of time. Also, it provides tax-free death benefits to the beneficiary. However, it has no cash-value or investment component.

What Insurance Policies Yield You Cash?

Permanent Life Insurance offers a cash value, it covers the life of the insured, and generally offers a consistent premium.

What Is Whole Life Insurance?

Whole Life Insurance pays dividends, it has a guaranteed cash value, and grows tax-deferred. Whole Life Insurance covers the life of the insured, and offers level premiums. Also, it pays death benefits to the beneficiary, which is usually income- tax free.

What Is Universal Life Insurance?
Universal Life Insurance offers flexible premiums, adjustable benefits, including a cash value. Also, it has a guaranteed interest rate, it grows tax-deferred, and it covers the insured for life. In addition, it pays death benefits to the beneficiary, which is generally income -tax free.

What Is Variable Universal Life Insurance?
Variable Universal Life Insurance is a cash value policy that you can borrow against. It offers flexible death benefits and premiums, and includes tax-deferred earnings. Also, it allows you to invest in a variety of investment vehicles. It is considered a good retirement vehicle for extra income.

An Important Note
In my opinion, if you choose any of the above insurance options you must keep your payments current in order to avoid any hassles or delays, if you should ever need to request a benefit payout.

What Is Annual Renewable Term Life Insurance?
An Annual Renewable Term Life Insurance policy is designed for short-term coverage. It offers the insured coverage for a set period of time, generally a 10 to 30 year life span. Premiums change yearly, and also rise, as the insured ages.

What Is An Annuity?
An Annuity is a great retirement investment vehicle, as it allows you an extra stream of income. With an Annuity, you can start receiving payments immediately, or defer payments for a later time. Also, Annuity payments are equal in value on a monthly basis. In short, there are two types of Annuities: fixed and variable, in which you have the option of requesting annual lump- sum payments.

What Is A Variable Annuity?
A Variable Annuity can be considered a risky business investment. However, it allows you to create retirement savings. Also, a Variable Annuity provides a guaranteed return , but the tax-deferred Annuity fluctuates on returns, and payment amounts are based on the performance of your investment portfolio. You can start receiving payments at a specified age or at the point of retirement.

What Is A Single Premium Deferred Annuity?
A Single Premium Deferred Annuity is a deferred annuity purchase that awards you a one-lump sum premium payment, which pays out a death benefit. Also, the annuity grows tax-deferred, until the time of allocation: an annuity is not tax deductible.

What Is Considered A Long-Term Insurance Policy?
A Long-Term Insurance Policy is a policy that provides long-term coverage for chronically ill and disabled persons. Also, this type of insurance covers the costs of long-term medical care expenses.

What Is An Accelerated Death Benefit Insurance Policy?
An Accelerated Death Benefit Insurance Policy can be added to your existing insurance policy, as a rider for an additional fee. You can receive cash advances, or borrow against the policy. When the insured dies, the balance of the policy is paid to the beneficiary. In short, this policy is good for terminally ill patients or persons receiving hospice care, because the policy allows the person to use death benefits to pay daily living expenses, including expenses for care.

Sources   Western and Southern Life
Western Union Assurance Company
U.S. Department of Health and Human Services
Internal Revenue Service
U.S. Securities and Exchange Commission
Wikipedia The Free Encyclopedia

Chapter Twenty-Two
Because Tomorrow Is Not Promised To Us
(Mathew 6:34 KJV)

This chapter covers the following topics:
Managing Your Money After Death
*Wills
*Living Will
*Codicil
*Executor Of Estate
*Power Of Attorney (Extent and Limitations)
*Trust
*Living Trust
*Living Revocable Trust
*Payable-On-Death Bank Account
*Transfer-On-Death Beneficiary (For married couples)
*Uniform Gift To Minors Act
*Joint Tenancy
*Tenancy By Entirety
*Joint Tenancy Bank Account
*Uniform Transfer-On-Death Securities
*Registration Act
*Marital And By-Pass Trust
*Qualified Terminal Interest Property Trust
*Charitable Reminder Trust
*Irrevocable Life Insurance Trust
*Beneficiary
*Trustee

What Is A Will or Last Will & Testament?

A Will or Last Will and Testament are a legal declaration, in which a person names an Executor to manage his or her estate after death. A will is the vehicle used to transfer a person's property after death, and it also lists beneficiaries, in which the property is distributed.

What Is A Living Will?

A Living Will is a legal document that is created by a person facing death. A living will can include what types of medical treatment you desire to be administered to you, if you are incapacitated; it gives the physician directives in how you want your last rights administered. In short, it guides your love ones on what to do concerning life prolonging treatments on your behalf.

What Is A Codicil?

A codicil is a modification of an existing Will. It is a legal instrument to add to a Will, revoke certain provisions of a Will, or to change a Will, all together. Drafting a codicil and then having it notarized, is usually not a valid execution of implementing the codicil. However, check with an attorney in your state to see what provisions you need to follow in drafting a codicil to your Will, as requirements vary from state-to-state.

An Important Note

In drafting a codicil to a Will, generally, it is required in many states as the Testator, you must "publish" the Will/codicil by declaring the document to be your last Will & Testament. If proper guidelines are not followed in accordance with your state's guidelines, the codicil is invalid. To me, the best way to change a Will, is to burn the existing Will and draft a new Will altogether. This way, leaves little room for questioning a Will's legitimacy. No one else should have the power to change your Will, but you.

Executor -Of-Estate

The primary responsibility of the Executor of Estate is to ensure your last Will & testament is carried out, and executed according to your wishes. The Executor of Estate is responsible for the following:

*Obtain certified copies of your death certificate.
*Locate the Will, as well as the beneficiaries.
*Examine/inventory safety deposit boxes.
*Attend your mail.

*Cancel credit cards and any subscriptions.
*Notify the Social Security Administration and all other business relations of your death.
*Oversee bank accounts, deeds, insurance policies, tax returns, and etc.
*Place notices in newspaper of your death.
*An Executor can also hire a probate attorney.

Administrator Of A Will
Generally, an administrator of a Will comes into play when the deceased has left no Will or the Will that was left was found invalid. However, generally, the administrator is appointed by the court before he or she can handle the decease's estate. If no one has been officially appointed, you can apply for a "grant of representation" with the Probate Registry in order to gain access to the decease's estate.

Power Of Attorney
It is when one person appoints another person to act on their behalf to execute decision-making power concerning one's finances and/or medical decisions. Generally, a person having Power of Attorney has the legal authority to make any decisions on your behalf, except write or change your Will. With a Power of Attorney, please make sure to specify its extent and limitations.

What Is A Trust?
A Trust or Trust Fund is an arrangement, in which property is managed by one person or a particular entity for the benefit of another person.

What Is A Living Trust?
A Living Trust is created and managed by the grantor, as he or she lives. It is generally created to save money on taxes or to manage property. It is also a legal document to ensure that the grantor's property is distributed, according to his or her wishes after death.

What Is A Living Revocable Trust?
A Living Revocable Trust is a legal arrangement, in which a grantor drafts to explain how he or she wants their property managed or distributed after death. Generally, the trust includes three parts: a grantor, a trustee, and a beneficiary.

What Is A Payable-On-Death Bank Account?
A Payable-On-Death Bank Account is a simple and inexpensive way to

put bank deposits and securities in a trust for your heirs. Also, a Payable-On-Death Account allows easy and quick access to your bank account at the time of your death. Generally, there is no cost to set up an account. Trusts are available at most banks, savings and loans, and credit unions, all you have to do is fill out the proper forms and name a beneficiary.

An Important Note
You can change a "POD" beneficiary at any time. According to Federal Deposit Insurance Corporation rule, POD accounts are insured up to $100,000 for each qualified beneficiary who is a parent, sibling, spouse, a child or grandchild. Also, a major benefit of the Payable-On-Death Bank Account is that it offers an easy way to transfer money after you die, without having to go through probate. **Currently, the District of Columbia and Fourteen (14) other states do not allow Transfer-On-Death Registration** of securities. They are as follows: Georgia, Hawaii, Indiana, Kentucky, Louisiana, Maine, Massachusetts, Michigan, New York, North Carolina, Rhode Island, South Carolina, Texas, and Vermont.

What Is A Transfer-On-Death Beneficiary?
The Uniform Transfer- On- Death Security Registration Act makes it easier to transfer securities when you die. It allows you to name a beneficiary to inherit your stocks and bonds, without having to go through probate. You can request a form that establishes a transfer of ownership of your securities/stocks or bonds by naming the person you want to receive your assets after death. Every state, but Texas has adopted the statue.

What Is A Uniform Gift To Minors Act?
The Uniform Gift to Minors Act (UGMA), which is adopted by most states, allows adults to transfer money and assets to minors, including setting up an account in the minor's name. The Act allows minors to own property and/or securities without having to establish a trust or having to retain an attorney.
*Second, the custodian has a fiduciary duty to manage the account, until the minor reaches the legal age of 18 or 21, depending on your state's statue.
*At which time the minor child becomes of legal age, he or she has the right to use the funds as he or she chooses, without any parental control. In other words, assets remain the legal property of the minor, and the

144

parent or guardian has no control over how the child spends the proceeds.

What Is An Accelerated Death Benefit?
An Accelerated Death Benefit allows the policyholder to receive a portion of his or her death benefits while they live. Generally, a percentage of the policy's face amount, discounted for interest, is paid to the policyholder prior to his or her death. Generally, benefits kick in if the insured becomes terminally ill, needs extreme medical intervention, must reside in a nursing home or can be used as the policyholder sees fit.

What Is Joint Tenancy?
Joint Tenancy is when both spouses share equal ownership of a specified property, which is automatically transferred to the surviving spouse when one spouse dies. Individuals, who are joint tenants not only share equal ownership of the property, they also have equal rights in what to do with the property. In short, a joint tenancy establishes a Right of Survivorship.

What Is A Tenancy In Common?
It is land or real estate owned by two or more individuals.
A Tenancy in Common is a less restrictive form of ownership that sometimes results when joint tenancies cease to exist, and Tenancy by the Entirety, which is a special form of joint tenancy for married couples.

Tenancy In Common
*It is an agreement that can be made between related or unrelated persons.
*Ownership of property can be of equal shares or unequal shares.
*Co-tenants can participate in ownership, if one of the common tenants warrants it. You do not need permission from the other tenants to share your percentage of the property with a co-tenant.
*Married couples can also participate in Tenancy in Common agreements.

What Are The Characteristics Of Joint Tenants?
Joint tenants share ownership of land. Nevertheless, property is also defined as money and/or other items.
*Joint tenants own an undivided interest in the property and each
 share is equal.
*The estate of the joint tenants is vested (meaning, fixed and unalterable by condition).
*Joint tenants hold the property under the same title.
*joint tenants have equal rights, until one dies. Under the right of

survivorship, the death of a tenant is automatically transferred to all survivors. When only one joint tenant is alive, he or she receives the entire estate. *If the joint tenants mutually agree to sell the property, they must equally divide the proceeds that originated from the sale.

*If one of the joint tenants decides to allow another to share interest in the property, the joint tenancy is broken and the new owner has what is called, tenancy in common.

*Tenancy in common is a form of concurrent ownership that can be created by deed, will or operation of law.

What Is Tenancy By the Entirety?

Tenancy By the Entirety is real property owned by a husband and a wife, which is created only by will or deed. Another form of joint tenancy creates a right of survivorship, which allows property to pass automatically to the surviving spouse. In addition, tenancy by the entirety protects a spouse's interest in the property from the other spouse's creditors. In the event of a divorce, the tenancy by the entirety becomes a tenancy in common, and the right of survivorship is lost.

What Is A Joint Tenancy Bank Account?

A **Joint Tenancy** checking or savings account is shared by a husband and a wife, if one spouse dies, the surviving spouse can continue to use the accounts as their own, without any legal Hassel.

Uniform Transfer-On-Death Securities Registration Act

The Act allows securities to be transferred to a beneficiary without having to go through probate or having to converse with an attorney. This is called registering the securities in beneficiary or transfer-on-death form. Every state, but Texas has adopted the statue.

What Is A Marital And By-Pass Trust?

A Bypass Trust allows married couples to shelter some of their estate from taxes. This type of trust is generally set up to leave assets and income to the surviving spouse. However, upon the death of the surviving spouse, trust assets are passed directly to the children, or other beneficiaries named without taxation. Other options to consider are gifts in trust, estate planning and distribution, and bypass trust.

What Is A Qualified Terminal Interest Property Trust?

A Qualified Terminal Interest Property Trust allows the grantor to provide for a surviving spouse after his or her death. The trust also discloses how assets are controlled or distributed, after the surviving spouse dies. In short, the trust, allows the grantor to provide income, security, and stability for the surviving spouse.

What Is A Charitable Reminder Trust?
A Charitable Reminder Trust provides the donor/guarantor income, as long as he or she lives. The trust allows the donor to donate money and/or property to a charity, while the donor also receives a steady income from the trust.

What Is An Irrevocable Life Insurance Trust?
An Irrevocable Life Insurance Trust owns and holds life insurance policies, on behalf of the grantor, which is deemed trust property. This type of trust was specifically created to exclude proceeds from taxable estate taxes upon the grantor's death. Once the trust is set up, you cannot alter the policy. The policy at this point is irrevocable. However, as the grantor, you can choose a beneficiary, set the terms in how benefits are distributed, as well as appoint someone to manage the trust after your passing.

What Are The Benefits In Having An Irrevocable Trust?
The benefit in setting up an Irrevocable Trust is that you can avoid estate taxes on life insurance proceeds by setting up a **"Generation Skipping Trust or Dynasty Trust,"** which can help you avoid estate taxes at each generational level for several years to come.

What Is A Beneficiary?
A beneficiary is a person or a legal entity, in which money or other benefits are left by a benefactor.

What Is A Trustee?
A trustee is someone who holds the title and trust for the benefit of another person and who owes fiduciary responsibility to that beneficiary. In short, anyone acting as guardian or fiduciary with respect to another person you can be both the owner and beneficiary of the life insurance policy. However, you cannot borrow from it.
Sources
Free Merriam Webster Dictionary
Wikipedia The Free Encyclopedia InvestorWords.com

"If you have a dream, believe it. If you have the will, do it.
I can, I will, I did."

- By IWIN-

Photo of Quentin DeAngelo Warren
An aspiring artist and Howard University Graduate of 2006

Chapter Twenty-Three
WRITE A LETTER WRITE A LETTER
SEND A MESSAGE SEND A MESSAGE
(A Human Nature Lyric)

This chapter covers the following topic:
A FREE SAMPLE LETTER SECTION for
CREDIT DISPUTES and NEGOTIATIONS
"FTC's mission is to protect consumers from fraudulent or deceptive claims that mislead consumers, and from harmful business practices that undermine the competitive process. The work of each of the agency's three Bureaus is unified behind this mission, and the Office of Policy Planning articulates the policy goals that support that mission," as defined by the Federal Trade Commission. *WARNING:* **"Always send dispute letters by official mail return receipt requested."**

How Can I Request My Free Credit Report?
Under The Fair Credit Reporting Act, you can request a free credit report from Experian, Equifax, and TransUnion credit reporting agencies. The author has provided the following sample letters for your convenience.

A FREE SAMPLE LETTER
REQUEST YOUR FREE ANNUAL CREDIT REPORT

DATE:_____

From:
Sender's Name _____
City and State_____
Zip Code_____

To:
Credit Reporting Agency (Experian, TransUnion and Equifax)
Address_____
City and State_____
Zip Code_____

To Whom It May Concern:

 I, (your name), am requesting my free annual credit report, as I am entitled to receive through The Fair Credit Reporting Act. Therefore, please send me the latest report from Experian, Equifax, and TransUnion credit reporting agencies. Also, as required by law, I have enclosed my Social Security number, date of birth, and current mailing address for the sole purpose of obtaining my free credit report.

Thank you in advance for your cooperation concerning this matter, as I look forward to receiving my complimentary credit report.

Respectfully,

(Your signature here)
(Your printed name here)
(Your initials here)

Also, you can request a free credit report by direct mail, telephone, and the Internet.
Send your written request to:
Annual Credit Report Request Service
P.O. Box 105281
Atlanta, GA 30348-5281.

Make your request by telephone
1-877-322-8228.

Make your request via Internet
at https://www.annualcreditreport.com/cra/requestformfinal.pdf, or
for additional information, please visit http://www.ftc.gov/freereports.

An Important Note
The "Federal Fair Credit Reporting Act promotes the accuracy and privacy of information in the files of the nation's credit reporting companies," as noted by the Federal Trade Commission.

Source
 Federal Trade Commission at
http://www.ftc.gov/bcp/edu/pubs/consumer/credit/cre21.shtm.

An Important Note
 "Your credit report contains information about where you live, how you pay your bills, and whether you've been sued or arrested or have filed for bankruptcy," as noted by the Federal Trade Commission. For more information, please visit the Federal Trade Commission at
http://www.ftc.gov/bcp/edu/pubs/consumer/credit/cre21.shtm.

Second, in addressing errors on your credit report, you can use the standard Federal Trade Commission sample letter provided for you by the Commission free of charge, or you can follow the various sample letters ranging from letter three –sixteen, in which the author has created for your convenience.

Sample Dispute Letter 2

Date
Your Name
Your Address, City, State, Zip Code

Complaint Department
Name of Company
Address
City, State, Zip Code

Dear Sir or Madam:

I am writing to dispute the following information in my file.
This item (identify item(s) disputed by name of source, such as
creditors or tax court, and identify type of item, such as credit account,
judgment, etc.) is (inaccurate or incomplete) because (describe what is
inaccurate or incomplete and why). I am requesting that the item be
removed (or request another specific change) to correct the
information.

Enclosed are copies of (use this sentence if applicable and describe
any enclosed documentation, such as payment records and court
documents) supporting my position. Please reinvestigate this (these)
matter(s) and (delete or correct) the disputed item(s) as soon as
possible.

Sincerely,
Your name

Enclosures: (List what you are enclosing.)

Source
Federal Trade Commission at
http://www.ftc.gov/bcp/edu/pubs/consumer/credit/cre21.shtm.

FREE SAMPLE LETTER
A REQUEST to HAVE ERRORS REMOVED
FROM MY CREDIT REPORT

DATE:_____

From:
Sender's Name _____
City and State_____
Zip Code_____

To: Credit Reporting Agency
Address_____
City and State_____
Zip Code_____

To Whom It May Concern:

I, (your name), am requesting that inaccurate data be removed from my credit profile. According to {list Name of the company here}, I owe {Amount here} on account number {list the account number here}.

For the record, this is not my account. Therefore, I am disputing the claim and thereby, requesting a full investigation into the matter. Also, as stated by The Fair Credit Reporting Act, which is enforced by the Federal Trade Commission, I am entitled, by law to have any error(s) removed from my credit profile.

In short, I have enclosed my Social Security number, date of birth, and current mailing address for the sole purpose in correcting this mishap. Please notify me in writing when errors have been corrected. Thank you in advance for your assistance concerning this matter. I look forward to hearing from you soon.

Respectfully,

(Your signature here)
(Your printed name here)

FREE SAMPLE LETTER
HOW TO REMOVE LATE PAYMENTS
FROM MY CREDIT HISTORY

TO: {List name of credit bureau: Equifax, TransUnion, Experian}

FROM: {Your name, address, state, city, and Zip Code here}

DATE: { Current date here}

SUBJECT: PLEASE REMOVE LATE PAYMENTS FROM MY
CREDIT HISTORY

I recently reviewed my credit profile and noticed that an old account still appears on my credit record. Therefore, I am submitting a written request, which is in compliance with The Fair Credit Reporting Act, Section 605 [15U.S.C.S1681C], **"Running of Reporting Period,"** to have the negative item (s) removed from my credit report.

Under the current law, adverse credit history is only allowed to remain on your credit record for a period of seven (7) years. However, I understand that some debts can remain on a person's credit record for a period of ten years, which does not apply to me, in this case. Therefore, as my circumstances meet the Running of Reporting Period clause, I ask that you honor my request by investigating my claim and make the necessary changes to have the negative information removed from my credit record in a time set forth by law.

[List account numbers of the accounts in questioned here]
Date account reported to credit Bureau_____
Name of the company that reported the account delinquent_____
Address of the company_____
Account type_____
How many days, months or years account exceeds the statue of imitations_____
Date account was open_____
Date account was suppose to be deleted from credit profile history

If you should have any questions, please do not hesitate to contact me at {your phone number here, or via email at {email address here}. Thank you in advance for your prompt attention concerning this matter.

I look forward to receiving an updated copy of my credit report as soon as it becomes available.

Respectfully,

(Signature here}
{Printed name here}

{Initials here}

FREE SAMPLE LETTER
An Adjusted Settlement Payment

DATE: [Today's date here]

TO: [Company's name and address here]

FROM: [Sender's name and address here]

SUBJECT: Paying off my account for a lesser amount. Requesting a confirmation and receipt.

Please send me a confirmation letter, in which your company agreed on [date agreement was made here] to accept a settlement payment of a lesser amount, instead of the initial amount owed. Also, as the recipient of my final payment, you agree to close my account in good standing, so that it does not affect my credit rating.

Thank you for your assistance concerning this matter. I look forward to hearing from you soon.

Respectfully,

[Your signature here]

[Your printed name here]

[Initials here]

FREE SAMPLE LETTER
A Final Payment Notification

DATE: [Today's date here]

FROM: [Your name and address here]

TO: [Name of the bill collector, and address here]

SUBJECT: [account number here]

Dear Sir or Madam:

Please be advised, I have enclosed a final payment of
$_____, as we previously agreed on [date, month, and year].
Also, the enclosed payment should bring my account to a zero balance,
which also concludes all business arrangements and/or obligations with
your company.

Please send me verification that you have received my final payment as
soon as it becomes available. If you have any questions, or should need to
contact me, please email at [list your email address here], or contact me
via telephone at [list number here].

Thank you in advance for your prompt attention concerning this matter.
I look forward to hearing from you soon.

Respectfully,

[Your signature here]
[Your printed name here]
[Initials here]

FREE SAMPLE LETTER
Stop Debt Collectors From Calling You

DATE: [List current date here]

FROM: [List the name and address of the sender here]

TO: [List the bill collector or agency's name and address here]

SUBJECT: **In response to your harassing and illegal calls (Stop it! It is Against the Law)."**

This is a **WRITTEN WARNING to "STOP CALLING ME!"**As pertaining to the FAIR DEBT COLLECTION PRACTICES Act, Section 805I [15 USC 1692c]: CEASE And DESEASE COMMUNICATION: legally, you cannot continue to contact me after I serve you this official notice. If you or anyone else representing your company continues to contact me after receiving this written notice, you will be in violation of the Federal Debt Collection Practices Act, under section 805(b). Please be advised that I will take every legal precaution available to stop you from harassing me.

Sincerely,

[Your signature here]
[Your printed name here]

FREE SAMPLE LETTER
An Expired Statute of Limitations Letter of Notification

DATE: [Here]

FROM: [Your Name and Address here]

TO: [Bill collector's Name and Address here]

SUBJECT: [The reason and action you want the agency or company to take here. Also, list your account number here]

Dear [Sir or Madam]

In response to your recent letter on [date, month and year],
[State the details of the letter and nature of the debt. Second, enclose any proof you might have as verification that you do not owe the debt, such as a receipt, a cancelled check, a money order, or billing statement.

I am writing this letter to inform you of my rights under the Fair Debt Collection Practices Act (FDCPA), and to let you know that the statue of limitations concerning this account has expired. Therefore, if you continue to contact me about this debt, which also lacks merit, places you in violation of the "The Fair Debt Collection Practices Act."

YOU HAVE BEEN WARNED, if you continue to harass me after this notice, I will have no other alternative, but to contact the U.S. Attorney General's Office and make him aware of the violation.

Sincerely,

[Your signature here]
[Your printed here]

SAMPLE LETTER
AN OPT-Out Letter To Have My Name Removed
From the Credit Bureaus' Marketing List

DATE: [List the current date here]

FROM: [List your name and address here]

TO: [List the name of Credit Bureau and the address here]

SUBJECT: **A Request to Have My Name Removed from the Credit Bureaus' Marketing List**

Dear Sir or Madam:

Please remove my name from your marketing list!
{List the reason that you want your name removed from the marketing list and any FTC laws that may apply here}. Thank you for your prompt attention concerning this matter.

Sincerely,

[Your signature here]

[Your Printed Name here]

[Your initials here]

An Important Note
To learn more, please visit the Federal Trade Commission at http://www.ftc.gov/privacy/protect.shtm. Also, FTC provides a brochure about consumer rights titled, **"Unsolicited Mail, Telemarketing and Email: Where to Go to "Just Say No!"**
You can call, or go online to download a copy at http://www.ftc.gov/bcp/edu/pubs/consumer/alerts/alt063.shtm.

A FREE SAMPLE DISPUTE LETTER

DATE: (List the current date here)

TO: (Name of credit bureau, mailing address, city, state, and zip code here)

FROM: (List account information here)

SUBJECT: A Request For Reinvestigation

I recently obtained a copy of my credit report, which I found the following account errors: {List the items you are disputing here}.

I am aware, under The Fair Credit Reporting Act, I am entitled to request a reinvestigation if there appears outdated, or inaccurate information on my credit record (list reason for re-investigation here).

Therefore, I am requesting an updated copy of my credit report reflecting these changes. Please mail me an updated copy of my credit report as soon as it becomes available.

Respectfully,

{Your signature here}
{Your printed name here}

SAMPLE LETTER
A REQUEST TO HAVE BILLING ERROR
REMOVED FROM MONTHLY STATEMENT

Today's Date:

From: [Your name and address here]

To: {Creditor's name and address here}

Subject: Please remove billing error from my monthly statement

---

Dear Sir/Madam:

I recently received my monthly statement and noticed that a billing error appears on my account. My account number is {Place account number here} {list item that is incorrect here} and {reason you believe the billing statement is inaccurate}.

I am requesting an investigation into the matter, as well as all inaccuracies be removed once the investigation has been completed. In addition, please send me an updated billing statement, which reflect the updated changes.

Thank you in advance for your prompt attention concerning this matter. I look forward to hearing from you soon.

Respectfully,

{Your signature here}
{Your printed name here}

-12-
SAMPLE LETTER
A REQUEST TO HAVE MY CREDIT REPORT
SEPARATE FROM MY SPOUSE

TO: {The name and address of the credit company here}
FROM: {Your name and address here}
DATE: {Today's date}
SUBJECT: {Requesting an individual credit report}

Dear Sir/Madam:

Please accept this letter as an official request to have my spouse's credit removed from my credit profile. I have enclosed my Social Security number, which is {place Soc# here} and also, I have provided a copy of my wife's Social Security number {spouse's name and soc# here} for the sole purpose of having our credit history individualized.

Please send me a copy of my updated credit profile as soon as it becomes available. Thank you for your prompt attention concerning this matter. I look forward to hearing from you soon.

Respectfully,

{Your signature here}
{Your printed name here}
{Your initials}

SAMPLE LETTER
A REQUEST to MERGE SPOUSE's CREDIT REPORT

TO: {Credit Bureau Name and Address here}

FROM: {Your name and address here}

DATE: (Today's Date)

RE: A request to have my spouse's credit history merged with mine.

Dear Sir/Madam:

Please accept this letter as an official request to have my spouse's credit merged with mine. I have enclosed my Social Security number {soc# here}, and the Social Security number of my spouse {list spouse's soc# here}. In addition, I have provided my credit report number for your convenience.

Please notify me as soon as the updated changes become available. Thank you in advance for your prompt attention concerning this matter. I look forward to hearing from you soon.

Respectfully,

{Your signature here}
{Your printed name here}
{Initials}

SAMPLE LETTER
A REQUEST FOR RE-INVESTIGATION

TO: {Name of Credit Agency here}

FROM: {Your name and Address here}

DATE: {Today's Date}

RE: Requesting A Re-investigation

To Whom It May Concern:

Previously, I sent you a request to have my account reviewed on {Date}, as I had previously questioned an inaccurate item that appeared on my credit report.

Still to date, the inaccurate information remains on my credit report. For the second time, I am asking you to investigate this matter and correct all inaccuracies. For your convenience, I have provided you a {list account numbers here}, {the amount}, and {the account date}.

In closing, please contact me once you have completed a full investigation into the matter. I look forward to receiving an updated copy of my credit report, which reflects the updated changes.

Respectfully,

{Your signature here }
{Your printed name here}
{Initials}

SAMPLE LETTER
A REQUEST to HAVE INCORRECT RE-APPEARING DATA
REMOVED FROM MY CREDIT RECORD

Dear Sir or Madam:

I sent you a written request on {date} to have an incorrect account removed from my credit profile. Recently, I reviewed my credit history and still, the incorrect data appears on my credit history.

Please be advised, this is a second request to have the incorrect data removed from my credit profile. Therefore, I am enclosing the necessary documentation in order to further investigate my claim and to update my credit profile. Please view the following information below:

{Please list the updated data here}

_____
_____
_____
_____
_____
_____

In closing, please send me an updated copy of my credit profile, which reflects the updated changes. Thank you for your assistance concerning this matter. I look forward to hearing from you soon.

Respectfully,

{Your signature here}
{Your printed name here}
{Initials here}

SAMPLE LETTER
A REQUEST to HAVE GOOD CREDIT RE-ADDED
to MY CREDIT HISTORY

TO: {Credit agency name and address here}

FROM: {Your name, address, and credit profile number here}

DATE: {Today's Date}

SUBJECT: A request to have good credit history re-added to my credit profile.

Dear Sir/Madam:

Recently, I reviewed my credit report and noticed many of my good-standing credit accounts have been removed from my credit profile. As I understand it, maintaining a good credit score is dependent heavily upon maintaining a positive credit history. Therefore, I am requesting the accounts mentioned below be re-added to my credit profile as soon as possible.

The accounts to re-add to my credit profile are as follows:
*Name of the creditor
*Account number
*Date that the account was opened
*Line of credit approved at the time account was opened
*Date that the account was paid in full.

In closing, please send me a copy of my updated credit report, which reflects these changes. Thank you in advance for your assistance concerning this matter. I look forward to hearing from you soon.

Respectfully,
{Your signature here}
{Your printed name here}

A SAMPLE CALL LOG
to Log Harassing Calls
Evidence in order to file a complaint with the police

Date	Time of Call	Company/person's Name	Number of Times Called

1._____

2.

_____

3._____

4._____

5._____

6._____

7._____

8._____

9._____

10._____

11. _____

12._____

13. _____

14._____

Additional notes:

_____

Photo: *public domain* "(George Washington, who presided over the convention, is the figure standing on the dais. The central figures of the portrait are Alexander Hamilton and Benjamin Franklin.)"

Chapter Twenty-Four

A CHAIN IS AS STRONG AS ITS WEAKEST LINK
(A saying dated as far back as C. Kingley7s letter on December 1, 1856)

This chapter covers the following topics:
The Preamble And The U.S. Constitution
The People's Role In Government?

The Preamble To The Constitution
"We the people of the United States, in order to form a more perfect union, establish justice, ensure domestic tranquility, provide for the common defense, promote the general welfare, and secure the blessings of liberty to ourselves and our posterity, do ordain and establish this Constitution for the United States Of America."

"Don't interfere with anything in the Constitution that must be maintained, for it is the only safeguard of our liberties."

-Abraham Lincoln-

The Bill of Rights
Amendments 1-10 of the United States Constitution

Amendment I
Congress shall make no law respecting an establishment of religion, or prohibiting the free exercise thereof; or abridging the freedom of speech, or of the press; or the right of the people peaceably to assemble, and to petition the government for a redress of grievances.

Amendment II
A well regulated militia, being necessary to the security of a free state, the right of the people to keep and bear arms, shall not be infringed.

Amendment III
No soldier shall, in time of peace be quartered in any house, without the consent of the owner, nor in time of war, but in a manner to be prescribed by law.

Amendment IV
The right of the people to be secure in their persons, houses, papers, and effects, against unreasonable searches and seizures, shall not be violated, and no warrants shall issue, but upon probable cause supported by oath or affirmation, and particularly describing the place to be searched, and the persons or things to be sized.

Amendment V
No person shall be held to answer for a capital, or otherwise infamous crime, unless on a presentment or indictment of a grand jury, except in cases arising in the land or naval forces, or in the militia, when in actual service in time of war or public danger; nor shall any person be subject for the same offense to be twice put in jeopardy of life of limb; nor shall be compelled in any criminal case to be a witness against himself, nor be deprived of life, liberty, or property, without due process of law; nor shall private property be taken for public use, without just compensation.

Amendment VI

In all criminal prosecutions, the accused shall enjoy the right to a speedy and public trial, by an impartial jury of the state and district wherein the crime shall have been committed, which district shall have been previously ascertained by law, and to be informed of the nature and cause of the accusation; to be confronted with the witnesses against him; to have compulsory process for obtaining witnesses in his favor, and to have the assistance of counsel for this defense.

AmendmentVII

In suits at common law, where the value in controversy shall exceed twenty dollars, the right of trial by jury shall be preserved, and no fact tried by a jury, shall be otherwise reexamined in any court of the United States, than according to the rules of the common law.

Amendment VIII

Excessive bail shall not be required, nor excessive fines imposed, nor cruel and unusual punishments inflicted.

Amendment IX

The enumeration in the Constitution, of certain rights, shall not be construed to deny or disparage others retained by the people.

Amendment X

The powers not delegated to the United States by the Constitution, nor prohibited by it to the states are reserved to the states respectively, or to the people.

Sources

NARA: The National Archives Experience
The Bill of Rights Institute
The Library of Congress

Understanding How The United States Government Operates On State and Local Levels Each state is sovereign. Meaning, each state has its own written constitution. This can include, police departments, schools or libraries, Secretary of State, and License Bureaus, which usually fall under state and local governments.

Understanding State Government
"Under the Tenth Amendment to the U.S. Constitution, all powers not

granted to the federal government are reserved for the states and the people. All state governments are modeled after the federal government and consist of three branches: executive, legislative, and judicial. The U.S. Constitution mandates that all states uphold a 'republican form' of government, although the three-branch structure is not required," as noted by the White House government website.

Understanding How The Executive Branch Works
"In every state, the executive branch is headed by a governor who is directly elected by the people--states reserve the right to organize in any way, so they often vary greatly with regard to executive structure. No two state executive organizations are identical," as noted by The White House government website.

Understanding How The Legislative Branch Works
"All 50 states have legislatures made up of elected representatives, who consider matters brought forth by the governor or introduced by its members to create legislation that becomes law. The legislature also approves a state's budget and initiates tax legislation and articles of impeachment. The latter is part of a system of checks and balances among the three branches of government that mirrors the federal system and prevents any branch from abusing its power," as noted by The White House government website.

The smaller upper chamber is always called the Senate, in which U.S. Senators serve a term of six years. Then, you have the U.S. House of Representatives, which serve a term of two years.

Understanding The Way The Judicial Branch Works
"The Supreme Court oversees the lower courts, in which they hear appeals from the lower courts. Court structures and judicial appointments/elections are determined either by legislation or the state constitution. The Supreme Court focuses on correcting errors made in lower courts and therefore holds no trials. Rulings made in state supreme courts are normally binding; however, when questions are raised regarding consistency with the U.S. Constitution, matters may be appealed directly to the United States Supreme Court, " as noted by The White House government's website.

Understanding How Local Government Works
"Local governments generally include two tiers: counties, also known as boroughs in Alaska and parishes in Louisiana, and municipalities, or cities/towns. In some states, counties are divided into townships. Municipalities can be structured in many ways, as defined by state constitutions, and are called, variously, townships, villages, boroughs, cities, or towns. Various kinds of districts also provide functions in local government outside county or municipal boundaries, such as school districts or fire protection districts," as noted by The White House government's website.

The White House via government defines
"Municipal governments — those defined as cities, towns, boroughs (except in Alaska), villages, and townships."

Who Oversees Emergency, Law Enforcement, Fire, Parks, and Recreation Services?
Municipalities oversee parks, recreations, the police and fire departments, housing services, municipal courts, transportation services, medical and emergency services.

An Important Note
The White House defines the powers of governments as, "the federal government and state governments share power in countless ways, a local government must be granted power by the state. In general, mayors, city councils, and other governing bodies are directly elected by the people."

Sources
The White House government website,
 Wikipedia The Free Encyclopedia

Census Bureau
www.census.gov

Consumer Information Center
www.pueblo.gsa.gov

Central Intelligence Agency
www.cia.gov

Consumer Product Safety Commission
www.cpsc.gov

Environmental Protection Agency
www.epa.gov

Equal Employment Opportunity Commission
www.eeoc.gov

Federal Communications Commission
www.fcc.gov

Federal Deposit Insurance Corporation
www.fdic.gov

Federal Election Commission
www.fec.gov

Federal Emergency Management Agency
www.fema.gov

**Federal Reserve System (FRS), Board Of Governors
Of The Federal Reserve Board**
www.federalreserve.gov

Federal Trade Commission (FTC)
www.ftc.gov

FedStats
www.fedstats.gov

Internal Revenue Service
www.irs.gov

National Transportation Safety Board
www.ntsb.gov

Postal Rate Commission
www.prc.gov

Search Gov
www.searchgov.com

Senate
www.senate.gov

Social Security Administration
www.ssa.gov

The Supreme Court
www.supremecourtus.gov

U.S. Commission on Civil Rights
www.usccr.gov

U.S. International Trade Commission
www.usitc.gov

U.S. Postal Service
www.usps.com

White House (The)
www.whitehouse

Chapter Twenty-Five

DEPARTMENTS OF GOVERNMENT ONLINE DIRECTORY

Vice President Of The United States
http://www.whitehouse.gov/administration/vice-president.com

Department Of State
http://www.state.gov

Department Of the Treasury
http://www.treasury.gov

Department Of Defense
http://www.defenselink.mil

Department Of Justice
http://www.usdoj.gov

Department Of the Interior
http://www.doi.gov

Department Of Agriculture
http://www.usda.gov

Department Of Commerce
http://www.commerce.gov

Department Of Labor
http://www.dol.gov

Department Of Health And Human Services
http://www.hhs.gov

Department Of Housing and Urban Development
http://www.hud.gov

Department Of Transportation
http://www.dot.gov

Department Of Energy
http://www.energy.gov

Department Of Education
http://www.ed.gov

Department Of Veterans Affairs
http://www.va.gov

Department Of Homeland Security
http://www.dhs.gov

THE CABINET-RANK LIST

White House Chief Of Staff
http://www.whitehouse.gov/administration/staff/

The Environmental Protection Agency
http://www.epa.gov

Office Of Management & Budget
http://www.whitehouse.gov/omb

United States Trade Representative
http://www.ustr.gov

United States Ambassador To The United Nations
http://www.usunnewyork.usmission.gov/

Council Of Economic Advisers
http://www.whitehouse.gov/administration/eop/cea/

Source
The White House Government website at
http://www.whitehouse.gov/administration/cabinet

INVESTMENT RESOURCE INDEX DIRECTORY

Purchase Real Estate Funds
Alpine U.S. Real Estate Securities
1-888-785-5578
www.alpinefunds.com

CGM Realty Fund
1-800-345-4048
www.cgmfunds.com

Fidelity Real Estate
1-800-343-3548
https://www.fidelity.com

Purchase Asset Location and Balance Funds
American Century Investments
1-800-345-2021
www.americancentury.com

American Funds Capital
1-800-421-0180
https://www.americanfunds.com/default-home.htm

Calamos Growth & Income Fund
1-800-582-6959
http://fundinvestor.calamos.com/MutualFunds/Fund.aspx?name=GrowthAndIncome.

Fidelity Convertible Securities
1-800-544-6666
http://personal.fidelity.com/products/funds/mfl_frame.shtml?316145200

Van & Kampen Equity Income A
1-800-847-8484
http://www.vankampen.com/AboutUs
http://www.vankampen.com/Products/MutualFunds/Overview/5596/A

Vanguard Wellington

1-877-662-7447

https://personal.vanguard.com/us/HomepageOverview?WT.srch=1

Vanguard Asset Allocation

1-877-662-7447

https://personal.vanguard.com/us/FundsSnapshot?FundId=0078&FundInt Ext=INT

All Business
www.allbusiness.com

e-Insurance Services Inc.
www.einsurance.com

Master Quote Of America Incorporated
www.masterquote.com

eHealth Insurance
www.ehealthinsurance.com

Tracking Consumer Reports For Financial Services
Track and compare insurance companies, brokers, banks, and any
financial institution at www.gomez.com

Mutual Funds
Provides information for over 9,000 Mutual Funds at
www.mutuals.com or valueline.com

Check The Backgrounds Of Financial Service Institutions
www.smartmoney.com

Real Estate Investment Trust
REITs are basically income securities
There are three types of REITs
(I found to be most promising)
*Mortgage REITs
*Equity REITs
*Hybird REITs

Mortgage REITs

*It is an investment trust in real estate, in which mortgage loans are granted.

*It is an investment loan secured by real estate.

*Revenue is generated from the mortgage interest and the principal.

Equity REITs

*Equity REIT is an investment trust in real estate.

*It is not a lender of real estate.

* It invests in properties and then, takes on ownership.

*Income is generated from rent.

Hybrid REITs

*It is an investment trust in real estate.

*Hybrid REIT lends money, plus takes on an equity position.

*It is an investment that includes both an Equity REIT and a Mortgage REIT, investing in properties and mortgages.

* It lends to mortgage borrowers.

*Income is generated from rent and capital gains.

Major Benefits Of Owning A REIT

*Own office buildings

*Own stores, and apartment buildings

*Own shopping centers, real estate, and more

*Receive special tax consideration

*Returns a high yield

WORDS of ENCOURAGEMENT

"Don't give up!" The only way to move up is to get up and continue trying. If you have your health and strength, and the love of your family and friends, I say you are rich already. All the best to you, and I will be praying for everyone who is fortunate enough to read this book.

"May God bless you all, and may God continue to bless the United States of America."

Irene is a motivational speaker and executive business coach in the Washington, D.C. area. If you wish to contact Irene for a one-on-one business consult, speaking engagement, or desire Irene to speak at a business seminar, college function or church seminar, please contact her via e-mail at itwarren@hotmail.com for additional information.

Alysia Ferrebee

Angela Thompson

Eugene H. Adams

Robert Alston

Barbra Bland

Thomas Brannum

Shahzad Chaudhry

George Hairston

Alysa Gillis (graphic and design)

Chico Hinton

Debbie Mitchell

Maynard Dixon

Joseph Parker

Joan Rodgers

Michelle Simms

Linda Satterthwaite

Maria Syrkes

Kevin Sewell

Anne Wallace

Isaac Wilson, Jr.

George Winstead

Why do I mention the persons who supported me, because I understand that no man is an island.

HAPPY LIVING

www.ingramcontent.com/pod-product-compliance
Lightning Source LLC
Chambersburg PA
CBHW051214200326
41519CB00025B/7116